Looking After Your
BOOKS

Looking After Your
BOOKS

Francesca Galligan

BODLEIAN
LIBRARY
PUBLISHING

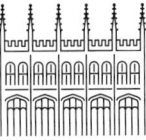

First published in 2025 by Bodleian Library Publishing
Broad Street, Oxford OX1 3BG
www.bodleianshop.co.uk

2nd impression 2025

ISBN 978 1 85124 627 4

Text © Francesca Galligan, 2025
This edition © Bodleian Library Publishing, University of Oxford, 2025

Francesca Galligan has asserted her right to be
identified as the author of this Work.

All rights reserved.

No part of this book may be reproduced, stored in a retrieval system, or transmitted in any form or by any means, electronic, mechanical, photocopying, recording, or otherwise, without the written permission of the Bodleian Library, except for the purpose of research or private study, or criticism or review.

Publisher: Samuel Fanous
Managing Editor: Susie Foster
Editor: Janet Phillips
Cover design by Dot Little at the Bodleian Library
Designed and typeset by Lucy Morton of illuminati in 10.6 on 15 Caslon
Printed and bound in China by C&C Offset Printing Co., Ltd.
on 130 gsm Chinese Yulong Cream Pure paper

EU GPSR Authorised Representative Logos Europe,
9 rue Nicolas Poussin, 17000, La Rochelle, France Contact@logoseurope.eu

British Library Catalogue in Publishing Data
A CIP record of this publication is available from the British Library

Contents

INTRODUCTION	1
Your Books as a Collection	5
How to Buy Books	34
Shelving and Storing Books	60
Conditions for Books	79
Common Conservation Issues	105
Ordering and Listing Your Books	119
Leaving Your Mark	133
Special Finishes for Special Books	151
Getting Rid of Books	164
END WORD	180
APPENDIX	182
INDEX	185

Introduction

IF YOU OWN BOOKS, and find yourself with practical questions about how to look after them or build on what you have, this book is for you. It will introduce you to collecting and buying books, and offer gentle guidance on how to shelve, protect and keep track of them, how to mark your ownership, and how to pass them on.

If you love books, you will find stories and curiosities drawn from the world of books, libraries and collecting across more than two millennia. You will be whisked from book crooks and forgeries, the finest Renaissance collections, and a jewelled binding that sank on the *Titanic*, to a reader worried about gout. You will meet Richard de Bury from the fourteenth century, who has much excellent advice on looking after books, Tudor queens who liked theirs bound in velvet, and ordinary book owners who make records of linen or deer or write poetry in their margins.

Perhaps you catch yourself occasionally wondering whether you are a book collector. Does your assortment of books that includes paperbacks, tattered volumes from childhood, dusty things picked up at jumble sales, a signed copy from a charity shop, and a special book given as a gift amount to anything as grand as a 'collection'? I think it does. There are many different ways of collecting, and some wonderful examples have been formed from everyday and inexpensive books. It is helpful to think of your books as a collection so that you can keep an eye on condition, avoid buying the same book twice and plan for future additions.

If you do own or collect books, do you keep them in the best condition you can? Perhaps you wonder how to dust them, or what to do with torn pages and crumbling spines. There is practical advice here on caring for damaged books in keeping with modern conservation standards. You will also learn about some dubious treatments used in the past, as well as oddities such as lip glue, waterproof book covers and medieval advice on not dropping crumbs in your books.

If you struggle to keep track of your books, and find yourself buying a second copy of something you already have, you might consider a list or catalogue. You'll be introduced to some historic examples and some modern equivalents. You might have a favourite book, and will find ideas here from past collectors about how to commission a special box or binding for it. I also think you should write in your books, but how might you do it sensitively, and what might you record?

Sometimes we find ourselves with more books than we can manage. Whether you are weeding your shelves or dealing with books from someone else's collection, the problem of how to get rid of them usefully weighs on many of us, and there are alternatives to a skip.

My experience as a rare book librarian at one of the world's great libraries lies at the heart of what I offer here. Librarians work closely with many others, and I would like to thank all my colleagues in Rare Books at the Bodleian – Alan Coates, Kate Guest, Katie Hannawin, Annabelle Hondier, Julie Anne Lambert, Jo Maddocks, Tessa Rose, Dunja Sharif, Sarah Wheale and Rob Wilkes – and Alice Evans, Samuel

Fanous, Andrew Honey, Janet Phillips, Alex Walker, Mike Webb and Daniel Butt for their guidance and generosity.

Your Books as a Collection

Do you consider yourself to be a 'book collector'? You might say yes, straight away. Many of us will hesitate; we own books, but don't really collect them. The term does not fit with what we buy day to day, or with the miscellaneous books we keep at home. What is the difference between a book owner and a book collector?

A book collector is actively looking for certain books, usually with a specific goal in mind, such as completing a set of something or acquiring anything relevant to a particular author, subject or collecting interest. But there is another perfectly valid way of collecting, which is simply to acquire whatever fascinates you, for whatever reason.

You might own books, and buy books for a specific purpose, but not think about them as a coherent whole, as something that can be cared for and expanded in useful or enjoyable ways. Whether you simply own or actively collect books, I encourage you to think of them as a collection. They don't need to be valuable, rare or even special to be thought of as such; they don't even need to make sense as a whole. But thinking of them in this way will help you to see what it is that you have and what you would like to have.

Thinking of collecting or expanding your collection?

Perhaps you do already collect books and are thinking of how to develop your collection further. Or you like books and are intrigued by the idea of a collection, but you are not sure where or how to begin. This chapter suggests ways in which you might start or develop a collection, with some notes about past collectors and collecting along the way to offer background, ideas and inspiration.

There are various reasons for collecting, or wanting to collect, and these have changed over the centuries. With the variety of books available today that go far beyond a merely practical use – that is, needing to read a text – there are all sorts of opportunities and reasons for collecting. Many collectors are driven by a simple love of books, by the author or subject they are collecting, or by the pleasure and satisfaction of setting a goal and working towards it. A collection can also be a financial investment, a reference library for a job or interest or hobby, material for leisurely reading, and memories of times and people past.

Collecting does not have to be expensive or time-consuming, though it could be both if that suits you. One of the wonderful things about books is that there is something available for almost any budget. You could pick up books destined for the bin – rubbish collectors in the Turkish capital Ankara opened a community library in 2018 of some 6,000 binned books – or splash out on something on sale for millions, and everything in between. If you do want to collect as an investment, or are planning to spend lots of money on books, you would do well to take advice from a reputable bookseller, and to familiarize yourself as much as you can with both the language of and the trade in rare books. There is more on this in the next chapter. There are many ways of collecting that do not seek out age or rarity for its own sake, but grow out of common and inexpensive contemporary books. As the collector Colin Franklin says in his essay 'Book Collecting as One of the Fine Arts', much of the fun in collecting lies in working out what to collect and then trying to find it.

How do you start?

BY AUTHOR/TITLE

Suppose you love Agatha Christie, and you own a handful of her works. You could form a collection around her in almost endless ways. Here are some suggestions.

You might start with acquiring a copy of each of her works, or a subset of these, such as her Poirot detective novels; an online search should bring up a chronological list of these. But before you start to seek them out, ask yourself what sort of collection you would like, as different editions offer different options. Do you want hardbacks or paperbacks? First editions? Do you want your collection to be neat and uniform? Who is it for? Yourself? Family? Does it need to hold value so that you can resell it?

HARDBACK/PAPERBACK

My household loves the sci-fi novels of Iain M. Banks. We have them all in paperback from the late 1990s and early 2000s, but we are slowly acquiring them in hardback. I say 'acquiring' rather than 'swapping', as we intend to keep both. The hardbacks are first editions from the 1980s and early 1990s from two different publishers, and offer different cover art (or, in later cases, modified cover art) and a solid and lasting presence on the shelf; but paperbacks are so much easier to read and carry around. I think it is acceptable to have more than one edition of a series of books that you really like.

But if you must choose, it depends on the sort of collection you want. First editions will usually be in hardback; hardbacks should be more robust and last longer, as the gatherings of leaves are stitched together then attached to the binding. Paperbacks are generally loose leaves glued into the spine, and over time will become detached. Hardbacks cost more to produce, and so will have a little more value than paperbacks. Do you prefer to look at a row of hardbacks or paperbacks? And do you have the space for hardbacks, which take up more room?

FIRST EDITIONS

Twentieth-century guides to collecting will instruct you to collect first editions (in hardback) with their original dust jackets. The difference in price between a first edition with or without its jacket can run to tens of thousands of pounds. Take *The Great Gatsby* by F. Scott Fitzgerald: a first edition without the jacket sells for around £7,000–£9,000; but with the original dust jacket, one of the loveliest with two mournful eyes emerging from an expanse of deep blue sky, the book sells for around £100,000, with one example fetching $377,000 in 2014. The gap in value between a first and second or later edition of a book can also be large, even when any differences between them are very minor. For example, the first edition of *Alice's Adventures in Wonderland* was printed in Oxford at the Clarendon Press and published in London by Macmillan in 1865. John Tenniel the illustrator was unhappy with the quality of the illustrations, and asked Lewis Carroll to have the edition reprinted. This was done in London later that year, and published with a title page dated 1866; the type was reset for this edition, and you can play a nice game of spot-the-difference with this and the edition of 1865, looking for differently spaced words, minor alterations to the layout and crisper illustrations. But what of the 2,000 or so copies that had been printed as the first edition? Carroll paid for new title pages to be printed and this was issued as the first American edition, also dated 1866, but with New York on the new title page. There are only twenty-two copies of the first edition still known, and if one were to come up for sale it would cost a lot. One came onto the market in 2016 with an auction estimate of $2–3 million, though it failed to reach the reserve price and was not sold. The London edition of 1866 also commands a fairly steep price (one sold in 2021 for $43,000). But the first American edition, which is exactly the same as the rare 1865 edition in all but its title page, sells for around £3,000. That's a lot of money saved for something that is – in all but one leaf – the same book.

People pay a premium for a first edition sometimes because it appeared in limited numbers and so is very rare, and sometimes because it is hoped that a first edition will always be alluring to future collectors as the first example of a work in print, and hold or increase its value.

How do you know if a book is a first edition? There is no straightforward answer, and working it out can, at times, be challenging. A few tips might offer a starting point. Some books state their edition on the title page or copyright page (usually on the back of the title page, but sometimes on a separate leaf); some might simply say 'First published…', and as long as this is followed by only one date it is probably a first edition. If a book has a date on the title page, and this date matches the copyright date, again you probably have a first edition. If there is no date on the title page, and just a copyright date, that is probably also a first edition. US editions often say when they are a first edition; UK editions often do not; but always keep an eye out for any sort of edition statement, whether on the title page or with the copyright information. Reprints by other publishers might repeat an edition statement, suggesting they are a first edition, but look out for clues that this is a later version, such as a different publisher listed on the binding, or cheap-looking paper. For older books, say, pre-1900, it is worth checking library catalogues to see whether you can find anything earlier than what you have (JISC Library Hub Discover, a free online catalogue that brings together the catalogues of major UK and Irish research and higher-education libraries, is good for UK publications, and the Library of Congress catalogue for American ones). Of course many books go through many editions in the same year, and to distinguish between these, if there is no edition statement (or date), you will need to consult a bibliography or secondary resource.

For books printed after about 1940, you can also look at the number that sometimes appears with the copyright statement, referred to as the 'number line' or publisher's code (not to be confused with the ISBN number). If it has a '1' in it, for example '10 9 8 7 6 5 4 3 2 1', this usually indicates a first edition (though not necessarily a first issue, which is another problem you might have to grapple with), and the 1 will be removed for the second edition. But there are exceptions, as publishers describe their editions in various ways; there are reference works that set these habits out for each publisher, and you might consult these before splashing out on something of which you are uncertain. Booksellers will also be able to help you with this; if you don't understand what they are describing, do ask. (There's more on this in the next chapter.) It can be very hard to distinguish between different editions and issues of a book, often coming down to a small mistake in the printing. For example, in the case of *Harry Potter and the Philosopher's Stone*, '1 wand' appears twice in the list of school items Harry must buy; this, alongside the publisher's name on the title page, the correct date and a '1' in the copyright line, confirms that it is a first edition, first issue. When you consider that there is often no significant variation between some editions, you might decide that you are happy with later ones that cost less and are more widely available, especially if you are collecting for your own pleasure rather than for monetary return.

APPEARANCE

If you want your collection of Agatha Christie to look good in a neat row on a bookshelf, then you might want to collect editions from a single publisher from a particular time, for example the slender green Penguin Books paperbacks that measure 18 by 11 cm. These later editions are nicely portable, easy to read in bed and take up much less room than a hardback edition. But you could pick any edition in hardback or paperback – including special or limited editions issued for anniversaries – and aim to gather a set of titles together. This sort of collecting, which has a finite goal, can be a good manageable project; you can add titles as and when you happen to come across them. Some collections of the works of a single author that have been donated to (or purchased by) the Bodleian include Kenneth Grahame, Edgar Wallace (with a film script of *King Kong*), Erasmus, Bruce Chatwin, Kierkegaard and Michael Moorcock. There is one female single-author collection of this sort there, a small group of books by Edith Sitwell, but there are other examples elsewhere of major authors of both sexes. If you are interested in knowing more, the index to the *Directory of Rare Book and Special Collections*, edited by Karen Attar, will direct you to them.

To return to Christie, and collecting by author or title, you could also pick your favourite work and collect every edition you can find, to see how it has changed over the course of its publication history; how cover art, layout, size, introduction and even title have changed at different times in different places. You could limit this by place, for example British or American editions, or by language, or have a combination of both, to show differences between editions published in different countries. P.G. Wodehouse's books often appeared under different titles in the USA, and we all know that *Harry Potter and the Philosopher's Stone* was published there as *Harry Potter and the Sorcerer's Stone*. Texts are not as unchanging as we sometimes imagine them to be.

This sort of collection can be particularly interesting for illustrated works. For example, you will recognize the original illustrations to Lewis Carroll's *Alice's Adventures in Wonderland* by *Punch* cartoonist John Tenniel that have become somewhat inseparable from the Alice stories. But when the British copyright expired in 1907, numerous illustrators took up the challenge: from Charles Robinson, with his beautiful black-and-white images; Gwynedd Hudson, who also designed posters for the London Underground; Willy Pogány and his short-haired Alice; to Salvador Dalí. Collecting illustrated editions of *Alice* provides a fascinating insight into changing fashions of book illustration over more than a hundred years; illustrated children's books are especially suited to this kind of single-title collecting. Similarly, you could collect by illustrator. There is a collection in the Bodleian that brings together the work of Arthur Rackham, from his bewitching and dream-like illustrations of goblins and fairies for classical fairy tales such as *Cinderella*, *Sleeping Beauty* and *Peter Pan* to the silhouettes of children at play that race over the endpapers of many of the books he illustrated. This collection aims to be as comprehensive as possible, including illustrations in lesser-known journals and editions in languages other than English, alongside the deluxe editions in their elegant publishers' bindings that command high figures from booksellers. A bibliography, which lists all known editions of an author or work, could be a good place to start with a collection such as this, and you might find – as with Rackham – that there are unlisted books out there waiting to be discovered.

Aside from Christie's novels, you could collect her plays or short stories, or move away from her writing entirely to collect reference works, critical literature and biographies of the author; other works of fiction that mention her; or even other works that use her characters. It could even be fun to recreate your own version of the private library of an author you love, though perhaps not Christie, as her family library held some 5,000 volumes. We have the surviving personal libraries (or lists of books) of many authors and historical figures, and these could be interesting to recreate in some form. The Bodleian has, for example, a significant part of the library of the philosopher John Locke, and of Robert Burton, author of *The Anatomy of Melancholy* (1621).

Elsewhere, you could explore libraries such as that of Jane Austen's family, at readingwithausten.com.

BY ASSOCIATION

There are other features one might also want to have as a basis for collecting. People like to own something that has a tangible connection to someone they admire. In the case of books, this could be one that belonged to the author in question, or a signed copy of one of their works. While authors have for centuries presented their books to others with dedicatory inscriptions, the idea of a signed copy is modern. Stephen King's finger, worn out with writing, apparently bled onto a book at one of his signings, and led to demand from the remaining queue that they too have a signature spotted with blood. According to the Guinness World Records, Vickrant Mahajan has signed the most books at a single event, managing to write in 6,904 copies of his *Yes Thank You Universe*, in 2016. The state of his fingers afterwards is not reported. There are different sorts of signed copies: presentation copies of the past were often speculative, sent in the hope of patronage, such as the Bodleian's copy of Tycho Brahe's book on astronomical instruments (*Astronomiæ instauratæ mechanica*, 1598) inscribed to the Doge of Venice; dedication and association copies are those inscribed by the author to close friends and family; modern signed copies are often done in bulk, as with Mahajan above, with or without an audience present, and to an unknown recipient. A copy signed by Christie is going to be expensive; collecting copies owned and inscribed by other interesting public figures whether or not they have a connection to Christie – or even by people otherwise unknown – will be more affordable, and will provide unexpected encounters that some people might prefer to a rigid set of collection goals.

BY SUBJECT

Christie's works could form part of a much larger collection by subject, such as detective fiction. As this would be vast without further boundaries, it could be narrowed down in any number of ways, by publisher, period, the type of author, where the stories are set, the social background of the detective, or anything else that takes your fancy.

You might already have a subject or theme in mind that relates to your profession or interests: books on plumbing, law, chess or trombones. Imagination can be given free rein here. The Maurice Ernest collection at the British Library focuses on longevity and old age, and the John Julian collection on eighteenth- and nineteenth-century hymnals. George Bowyer presented his collection of statutes of Italian cities to the Bodleian; Ingram Bywater his collection of books showing the history of classical learning; Strickland Gibson his collection illustrating the stages of producing printed books; and E.T. Long his collection of leaflets on English parish churches. The Bodleian has the Jessel collection of books about games of cards, chance or fortune-telling, and the Dummett collection complements this with books about twentieth-century card games. Johns Hopkins University's Bibliotheca Fictiva collection is dedicated to textual forgeries; the Harry Price Library of Magical Literature is kept at Senate House Library; and the Lisa Unger Baskin collection at Duke University celebrates the work of women.

Collect books about female explorers, and narrow these down by time or location. Or seek out books about the place where you grew up; the more obscure that place, the more of a challenge – and fun – you will have in finding relevant books. The edges to this sort of collecting are less well defined, and, even though available bibliographies might surprise you, serendipity will play more of a role. And that is what can make collecting so enjoyable.

Library catalogues can help you to work out whether there is a bibliography of the subject you are interested in: again, the JISC or the Library of Congress catalogues are good places to start, with keywords such as 'bibliography' and the name of author, illustrator or topic.

To whet your appetite, here are a few examples of some unusual bibliographies that offer a starting point for a specialized collection:

Otto Penzler, *An Annotated Bibliography of First Editions of Mystery Fiction Set in the World of Books, 1849-2000*
Joan Newman, *Girls Are People Too! A Bibliography of Non-traditional Female Roles in Children's Books* (1982)
Alberto D'Elia, *A Bibliography of Italian Dialect Dictionaries* (1940)
Roger Burt, *Bibliography of the History of British Metal Mining* (1988)
Grace Greenleaf Ransome, *Puppets and Shadows: A Selective Bibliography to 1930* (1997, on puppet plays)
Felicitee Sheila Forrester, *Ballet in England: A Bibliography and Survey, c. 1700–June 1966* (1968)

George Bridge, *Rock Climbing in the British Isles, 1894–1970: A Bibliography of Guidebooks* (1971)
Catherine Townsend Horner, *The Single-parent Family in Children's Books: An Annotated Bibliography* (1978 and 1988!)

BY PLACE OR LANGUAGE

You could collect by place of printing, whether somewhere unusual or special to you. There is a collection in the Bodleian devoted to books printed in Malta. Many bibliographers have arranged their catalogues of early printing by place; even a recent work on female printers of the sixteenth century (Axel Erdmann, *My Gracious Silence*) arranges them by the city in which they were based. Grouping books by printing place helps us to make comparisons within and between different local centres of book production, and in the past helped to identify works that do not give a place or printer's name.

You could also collect by language. Douglas Bartlett Gregor collected some 800 books in Esperanto, now in the Bodleian, and the Charles Leland collection at the British Library gathers books on Romany peoples and their languages. Early in the seventeenth century the

Bodleian acquired books in Chinese and Japanese that no one at the library, in Oxford or even England at the time could read. Thomas Bodley and his first librarians and benefactors recognized that these books deserved a place in the library, and that scholars with the relevant language skills would one day be able to read and benefit from them. Later that same century, the librarian Thomas Hyde was able to engage a Chinese visitor, Sheng Fuzong, to shed light on these collections.

BY PUBLISHER OR SERIES

Focusing on a particular series or edition or printing house is another way to collect. We are probably all familiar with the Folio Society, but what about the many private presses – that is, small, usually artisanal outfits producing elegant volumes in limited editions from the late nineteenth century onwards. Some, such as the Kelmscott Press of William Morris, are high end and much sought after; but there are plenty of others that would make an interesting and affordable collection. The best way of getting to know these sorts of books is by seeing examples for sale. There are also general guides to and bibliographies of the most well-known private presses.

FORMAT AND GENRE

You could collect by format: books in more unusual shapes such as tall thin books in 'wallet' format, round or heart-shaped books (some beautiful examples of these survive from the fifteenth and sixteenth centuries) or miniature books. The Bodleian's Morton collection of miniature books always delights those who see it, and the many bibliographies – and a thriving trade – are testament to the popularity of small formats with collectors. Some of the smallest books in the Bodleian are a tiny volume of sermons written in shorthand around 1650 and kept on a wooden rod by a silver chain for fear it be carried away by a mouse, and a German ABC from 1971 that was for a while officially the smallest book in the world at 3 × 2.5 mm. Publishers have, for a long time, issued some of their most popular titles in small formats, from the editions of poetry issued in Venice in the 1510s and 1520s by Alessandro Paganino that are 10 cm high, to the works of Shakespeare published by Allied Newspapers around 1930, in forty volumes 5 cm high and in their own wooden bookstand. My own favourites, most of which are not technically miniature, as they exceed 10 cm in height, are those that make up the 'travelling library' presented to a young Prince Charles (later Charles I of England) around 1609. These sixty small books were gathered together and bound in matching red goatskin with gold tooling, to be presented to the prince as a lavish gift. There is discussion of special bindings for special books in Chapter 8.

You could also collect by a combination of genre and format, such as photobooks, comics, facsimiles of precious old books, concrete poetry or zines. You can move beyond conventional ideas of what a book is to include the work of artists that challenge these: how about a book made of slices of cheese (this exists, but is very impractical), or a replica of an Elizabethan ruff made of small volumes of Shakespeare, or a book that self-destructs on reading. Printed ephemera – that is, printed items that were not intended to be kept, such as menus or tickets or advertisements – are another option. The Bodleian has one of the largest collections in the world of these transient pieces of printing, including one of only two copies of an advertisement by the first printer in England, William Caxton, advertising a handbook for priests around 1477.

BINDING

Many collections have also been put together around particular types of binding. There is endless scope here for different budgets, from lavish Renaissance bindings to modest twentieth-century cloth ones. The British Library has the Olga Hirsch collection of books in decorated paper wrappers, and the Bodleian the Carter collection of nineteenth-century publishers' bindings, as well as collections of expensive high-end bindings of different periods. Bindings are made of all sorts of different materials, including silver or other metals, animal skin preserved in different ways and from different animals (calfskin, goatskin, pigskin, sheepskin, deerskin, shark or ray, and elephant are all found in the Bodleian, but I know of books bound in seal, zebra and kangaroo), paper (decorated, a certain colour, printed, waste being reused), textile (cotton, linen, silk, velvet), straw. And they are decorated in countless ways (painted, tooled, embroidered, beaded, enamelled). Selecting a type of binding to collect will depend on your budget and tastes. A sixteenth-century painted vellum binding will be expensive and hard to find, but there are vellum bindings available that were painted and sold to tourists in Italy around the turn of the twentieth century. You could start with an ideal collection in mind, and adjust it downwards to match your budget. I love velvet bindings, the favourites of Tudor monarchs, and bought a dull book, a life of Christ in German, because its binding of red velvet with silver embroidery reminded me of a Bible in the Bodleian bound in red velvet and embroidered with silver thread and seed pearls for presentation to Elizabeth I. A sixteenth-century embroidered one would be prohibitively expensive for all but a few; a nineteenth-century German one, picked up at a market stall, was reasonable at £10.

Clean/used copies?

Most books on collecting will tell you to look carefully at the condition of a book you are thinking of buying, as this greatly affects its value. They will tell you to choose copies without obvious signs of damage or loss, still in their dust jackets, that are 'clean' – that is, without inscriptions (unless they are that of the author, or someone famous) or notes written in the margins (unless they are by the author or someone famous). Even then, past collectors and even libraries have liked to erase notes that we would now think of as important, in pursuit of the 'clean'. The Bodleian has a copy of Fanny

Burney's *Camilla* that was owned by Jane Austen. She wrote a note at the end of the book in pencil, on what a relief it was for Camilla that Mr Marchmont had died; the pencil has become very faint, and part of the note was cut away by a careless later binder. Clean and pristine copies might be easier to sell, if that is the main purpose of your collecting; but copies that show signs of use have much to offer.

You could collect copies where people have written in the margins, even if these are modern, and not by anyone recognizably famous. Marginalia is a field of ever-growing interest and scholarship, with people deciphering marginal comments that tell us something of how books were read or used in the past, whoever their owners were. Copies of modern books full of highlighter and biro might not be your idea of a nice book, and you wouldn't want to pay anything much for one. But they can often be rather fun, as the public Facebook group Oxford University Marginalia shows with its frequent postings of amusing comments spotted by readers in library books. There is more on marginalia in Chapter 7. You might even get lucky, and find something annotated by someone of note that has escaped everyone's notice.

Some past collectors

Although most attention has been given to male collectors of the past, there have been many female book owners, some of whom actively collected. Frances Wolfreston, a well-off but non-aristocratic woman, purchased modest volumes of contemporary English literature in the first half of the seventeenth century. She wanted to build a library for herself and her family, and provide them with literature, educational works and books for private devotion. What was for her and her contemporaries a collection of everyday books – the sort of English literature that Thomas Bodley called 'rifferaffe and baggage books' and deemed unsuitable for a scholarly library such as the Bodleian – has survived for four hundred years and become the most astonishing collection of rarities. The only surviving copy of the first edition of Shakespeare's *Venus and Adonis* (1593) is hers. Similarly, Cary Coke, an aristocratic woman from the late seventeenth/early eighteenth centuries, collected contemporary English plays, binding them up together into multiple volumes, and marking them proudly with her bookplate. She shared some of these with her husband, using a different bookplate that names them both.

Before institutional and public libraries were widely established, many private collectors saw their books as a resource for family, friends and scholars. Some even labelled them to suggest this sense of sharing. Inspired by his French counterpart Jean Grolier, the sixteenth-century English collector Thomas Wotton had fine bindings made for his books with his name and *et amicorum* – that is, 'and friends' – tooled in gold on the covers, and the phrase was used in inscriptions by many book owners of the period. Books were a precious resource, and, if one was lucky enough to own some, sharing or allowing access was encouraged. The Italian poet Petrarch had a large personal library of manuscripts in the fourteenth century, and shared them closely with his friend and fellow poet Boccaccio. Some of the books that survive from his library were annotated by both men, apparently sitting side by side.

Personal libraries often became the foundation of institutional and public collections: that of Henry E. Huntington, whose fortune came from railways, is the basis of the Huntington Library in San Marino, California; the Pierpont Morgan Library in New York was once the private library of the financier J.P. Morgan; and Henry and Emily Folger's books, purchased with oil money, was the foundation of the world's largest Shakespeare collection, now in Washington DC.

Modern collecting (on a budget)

Some modern collectors of books include Ian Fleming, who established a journal devoted to this subject, and George Lucas, whose 27,000 volumes now make up the Lucasfilm Research Library, but excellent collections can be put together on a lesser budget.

Many institutions and booksellers now offer book-collecting prizes, and the entries for these are a good source of inspiration. Usually put together with limited student finances, these are often extraordinary in their creativity and focus. What about a collection of books secretly funded by the Foreign Office to promote Western democracy over communism? This won Musa Igrek the 2018 Anthony Davis Book Collecting Prize, along with Lucy Vinten Mattich's collection of books of household management, 1760–1960. Or Berlin 2001–2010, as seen in photographic books (collected by Sylee Gore, winner of the 2020 Colin Franklin Prize). These winners of the prize offered by booksellers Honey & Wax for female collectors also offer food for thought:

Melanie Shi, for translations of ancient and modern Chinese works marketed by European publishers during the Cold War; Elsie Birnbaum's collection of Girl Scouts handbooks and official publications; Francesca Mancino's collection of modernist but forgotten women writers and publishers; Ariana Valderamma's collection of books relating to Toni Morrison's work as editor and reviewer; Miriam Bordern's collection of twentieth-century Yiddish primers and workbooks for children; and Emily Forster's collection of fan-made self-published comics. Other honourable mentions for this prize include collections on black equestrian history (Caitlin Gooch); the American vegetarian movement, 1971–present (Julia Fine); fairy tales from the nineteenth century to now that connect classical tales to a particular historic moment (Stacy Shirk); and twentieth-century travel guides for Russia, the Soviet Union and the Eastern Bloc (Caitlin Moriarty). There are many more examples in the blog posts on Honey & Wax's website about this prize.

Having said all this, unless you are preparing to spend significant sums of money, buying books you like, for whatever reason, is a good way to collect. Sets of things, matching books and completeness appeal to some of us, but others prefer to collect in a more general and serendipitous way. We are all collectors of a sort, and a collection could simply be an assemblage of books you like. I'm not proposing to form a collection of embroidered bindings, but the velvet one I mentioned above is part of my miscellaneous grouping of books that remind me of other books I like very much. By keeping an eye out, and being inventive in what you acquire, you will find 'old' or interesting books that are both affordable and pleasing to own, and appeal to you in ways that are unexpected.

How to Buy Books

Once you have some ideas about what to collect, how do you go about acquiring books? Will you seek out specific books online with bibliographies or reference works on hand; do you have hours to browse; or will you let serendipity play a role? While our first instinct in the twenty-first century might be to reach for an electronic device and search online – and this is great if you know exactly what you want – there are other more enjoyable ways of browsing and acquiring books. Of these, bookshops and book fairs come top of the list.

Bookshops and booksellers

A simple online search for 'bookshop' (for example, on Google maps) will show what's nearby in many countries around the world. If you want antiquarian bookshops, national and international antiquarian booksellers' associations will help you with this. In the UK, the website of the Antiquarian Booksellers' Association has over 230 members, and shows a map of members' shops, including those that sell general second-hand material. Of course not all sellers are members, so only one of the more than a dozen bookshops at the famous 'town of books' Hay-on-Wye is included. If you haven't been, this charming village on the Welsh/English border became a centre for second-hand and antiquarian books in the 1960s. You can find similar book villages or towns crammed with bookshops in France, such as Montolieu in the south, where you can pick up plentiful eighteenth-century books for €10 a piece; or Charlottesville, Virginia, in the USA, where the local Rare Book School furnishes a steady stream of buyers and browsers.

The International League of Antiquarian Booksellers also has an online list of its members. Buying from a seller registered with one of these organizations will offer some peace of mind for the buyer, as membership involves adhering to a code of ethics and professional standards that will help to ensure what you buy is legitimately for sale and as you expect it to be. These standards include the requirement for an accurate description that includes a book's defects and any restoration; diligence in checking against stolen property; a requirement not to break books or manuscripts up to sell as single leaves or prints; and a full cash refund, including postage, if the book is not as described.

Another plentiful source these days is the charity shop. The National Trust, Oxfam and Amnesty International all have dedicated second-hand bookshops, and most other charity shops have at least some books. Oxfam bookshops often include rare and antiquarian books, signed editions of modern books, and out-of-print and specialist modern books. Occasional treasures turn up too, such as the first edition of Harry Potter picked up for 50p at a charity shop and sold at auction for £15,000 in 2022. I've also heard of a dictionary full of notes in the margins in the hand of J.R.R. Tolkien that was picked up some years ago in my local Oxfam shop. While you won't tend to find many antiquarian books in regular charity shops, I saw a leaf from a medieval manuscript purchased for £7 last year from one local to me. I've found nothing so exciting, but I am still annoyed with myself for not buying a very lavish modern binding by one of the finest of fine binders – the London-based Sangorski & Sutcliffe – that was on sale in my local Oxfam bookshop. It even had beautiful endpapers depicting water lilies, but I didn't buy it because it seemed extravagant at £60, and the text was not of immediate appeal. My ongoing regret about this could be turned to your advantage, and you could succeed where I failed: if you find something you wouldn't normally buy, which is of excellent quality, and you like it either as a text or as an object, and could afford it, don't hesitate!

Antiques shops and markets, flea markets and car boot sales also offer opportunities for buying interesting books if you have some time to rummage thoroughly and visit often. I browse my local weekly outdoor antiques market, and, though I usually leave without anything, a handful of interesting purchases make up for these mostly disappointing trips. My best buys include a first edition (first issue) of Byron's *Marino Faliero* and *The Prophecy of Dante* for £10. Current prices on AbeBooks for this issue vary from £45 to £1,556, depending on whether all pages are present, general condition and the quality of the binding. Another book I was pleased to snap up was a compilation of questions about popular biology and natural history that goes under the title of *Problems of Aristotle*, or *Aristotle's Masterpiece*. I picked up an edition of this work from 1682, cheap because it was missing its title page and therefore without a date. I hadn't been a rare book librarian for very long at that point, but I had a hunch it was seventeenth century, so I bought it. Only two other copies of that edition are known. It was a bargain at £20, as these typically sell for several hundred pounds when complete, but here is the problem: condition, for most collectors, is everything. Many serious collectors would not want a copy such as this that was lacking its title, and nor, generally, would research libraries. So the market for this sort of imperfect book is small, but as I like curiosities, and don't want to spend a great amount on what I buy, this kind of find suits me well. There are some thoughts on imperfect books in Chapter 7.

So visit such shops and stalls often, and act on a hunch: not that something might be valuable, but that it might be rare, interesting or special; and, most importantly, because you like it.

Book fairs

Book fairs are a great opportunity to browse all kinds of books and see things you might not otherwise encounter. They help to give a sense of the market and prices for certain kinds of books and, perhaps most importantly, they provide opportunities for handling books. This is so much more useful, not to mention enjoyable, than trying to buy something based on online images where material forms (and important aspects such as scale) are often lost. A friend once purchased an accordion online, and was disappointed to find, on its arrival, that it was a miniature model of one. Online, all accordions – and books – look the same size, so seeing the real thing is always preferable.

Fairs dedicated to the sale of books have been around in Western Europe since the late fifteenth century, though books were sold at general fairs and markets for a long time before then: Socrates mentions books for sale at the market in Athens. They have been a main source for booksellers' stock and for collectors for centuries, and today offer an excellent way into collecting. In the seventeenth century the twice-yearly Frankfurt Fair was opened with bell-ringing and pageantry, and attended by booksellers, printers, agents and scholars from around Europe. New editions were offered there alongside a selection of older ones. The French printer and scholar Henri Estienne wrote a poem in praise of the fair in 1574, calling it the 'Frankfurt Athens'. The fair was even used as a cover for a secret trip down the Rhine by the exiled Charles Stuart (later Charles II of England) with his friends and sister the Princess of Orange. Fairs are now separated into what we might call trade fairs, where publishers promote and sell rights to their new stock, as they also did at Frankfurt, and antiquarian, second-hand or special-interest fairs, where older, collectible and more unusual books can be found. We are concerned primarily with the latter, which range from provincial fairs – for example, those organized by the Provincial Book Fair Association, where books cost anything from a few pounds upwards, or specialist ones, such as the Oxford Fine Press Book Fair – to the grander national fairs run by antiquarian booksellers' associations, such as the London Antiquarian Book Fair, currently known as Firsts.

What happens at a book fair? A range of people frequent them: collectors, book dealers, librarians, celebrity patrons and collectors (David Attenborough opened the London fair in 2018, and Stephen Fry in 2019), students, and above all people who like books. There is usually a small entrance fee, often avoided by downloading a free ticket from the fair website in advance. Booksellers set up stalls with shelves and tables that offer a selection of their stock that can be browsed and handled. There will also be items in glass cases. At provincial fairs these tend to be small books that might more easily go astray; at major antiquarian fairs glass cases will hold the more expensive books. In both instances sellers will be happy to show you these items. There is no particular pressure to buy, and sellers will occasionally offer a slight discount. I'm shy about this, and never ask; you might find it second nature, and a simple 'Is this your best price?' might do. Dealers conduct a lot of their own business at book fairs, buying each other's stock. They offer each other a trade discount, so don't feel put out if you see someone else getting a much better price than the one on display, as the customer might be another bookseller.

You can get to know booksellers at fairs. Tell them the sort of thing you are interested in, and these specialists can help you find the sorts of books you want, open your horizons to new material and offer advice on building collections. It might seem daunting to approach a stall where books are on sale for tens or hundreds of thousands of pounds (or even millions, such as the Copernicus on sale in 2023 at the London fair), but most sellers will have a range of stock including cheaper and more affordable books, and will be keen to meet new collectors. If Bernard Black from Black Books is etched in your mind as a model of a bookseller, rest assured that real-life examples are usually much more helpful.

You can find calendars of fairs on the websites of the Provincial Book Fair Association (for the UK) and the International League of Antiquarian Booksellers, which lists fairs of its members around the world.

Auctions

> It hath not been usual here in England to make sale of books by way of auction, or who will give most for them: but it having been practised in other countreys to the advantage both of buyers and sellers; it was therefore conceived (for the encouragement of learning) to publish the sale of these books this manner of way.
>
> William Cooper, *Catalogus variorum & insignium librorum instructissimae bibliothecae… Lazari Seaman*, 1676

English audiences were introduced to book auctions in 1676, with this sale of the books belonging to the deceased clergyman Lazarus Seaman. The sale took place in Seaman's house, and continued daily until all the books were sold. William Green Junior gives us an idea of what some of these early book auctions might have been like, with his *A Scene at an Oxford Book Auction*. This painting of 1747 shows a room with shelves of books reaching up to the ceiling, an auctioneer on a podium in the corner, and thirty or so men wearing wigs, mortar boards and velvet coats, perusing the books on sale. By contrast, an image of a street auction from around 1700 shows a smartly dressed dealer behind a table of books set out under a tree in Moorfields in London.

Auctions were sociable events, and often held on more than one day. That of Martin Folkes in 1756 stretched over forty days, and it took sixteen different multiple-day sales in three cities to sell the 200,000–300,000 books of Richard Heber between 1834 and 1837. The catalogues of these sales have great historical value, and are often collected now in their own right. After the sale, you could have your copy marked up by the bookseller with the prices and names of the buyers, and these records provide important evidence for the history of collecting.

Auctions might also seem daunting, but, like book fairs, they cater for a range of budgets and offer interesting books. This is where booksellers get much of their stock. You don't need an intention to buy anything or proof of wealth to attend an auction, even those of medieval illuminated manuscripts at leading auction houses where most items are listed at hundreds of thousands of pounds. It's quite an experience to attend, and, even though many now take place online, I would encourage you to go to a live one if you have a chance. Even with bids coming in remotely or online, they are still exciting. There are confusing aspects, not least unsold lots (where the reserve price hasn't been met), and fees to look out for, such as the buyer's premium, often an extra 30 per cent added on top of the hammer price. Books are laid out for viewing before the sale, and this is a good time to visit and browse and handle any books, whether or not you are intending to bid. You will have to sign up or register as you go in, and you'll be given a paddle whether you want one or not.

The first one I went to was as a graduate student learning about medieval manuscripts. I thought I'd better get dressed up, in case my impoverished student status kept me from entering the saleroom. The point is nobody is turned away from even the grandest of auctions, and no one will ask you what you do or how much money you have before letting you in. I sat on my paddle, convinced that my arm would rise up of its own accord as the bidding for an illuminated manuscript crept up and beyond £1 million. I had picked an exciting first auction, though the auction record for a manuscript is $38.1 million, for the oldest surviving Hebrew Bible, known as the Codex Sassoon, sold at Sotheby's in May 2023. Before that the record was the $30.1 million paid by Bill Gates in 1994 for Leonardo da Vinci's collection of scientific writings known as the Codex Leicester (or Hammer).

Sale lists and catalogues

Items at auction are listed or catalogued in advance, and these are also good to browse. Doing so was in fact a necessary part of a librarian's job in the seventeenth century, as it still is today. Rule 4 for actions that were to be taken by Bodleian library staff in the 1660s was

> That the catalogues of auctions at home & beyond sea as they come forth shall be examined and the names of all books of value, not in the library, be delivered in to the vice-Chancellor and Delegates, before the auctions begin.
> *Curators' Minutes Book*, 1678–1770

Most of these listings are now available online; you can sign up for notifications of these via the auction houses' websites. The glossy printed catalogues of the high-end auction houses that used to accompany such sales now only appear for a handful of special collections, and, as before, can be purchased in advance.

As well as auction catalogues, booksellers' catalogues will be invaluable in your search for books. These have fixed prices for the books on offer, rather than auction estimates. Many booksellers issue regular printed or electronic catalogues of selections of the books they have for sale and will be happy to add you to their mailing lists and send catalogues for free. Even as early as the fifteenth century booksellers printed stock lists on single sheets of paper, and pinned them up on walls for customers to peruse. A handful of examples – all very rare – survive from that period, such as the list of books on canon law offered by an itinerant bookseller in Germany in about 1476. The printer left blank the name of the place in each town where books could be bought, so that individual sellers could add their own details. The Bodleian's copy has the name added of what is probably the inn where the books were temporarily available, and has holes in it from where it was fixed up as a poster.

The Frankfurt Book Fair issued catalogues of what was on offer, and English booksellers soon produced their own version of the Frankfurt lists with books thought particularly useful for an English market. Scholars, writers and institutions of the time – including, in the seventeenth century, Robert Burton, the Bodleian Library and Tobie Mathew, the Archbishop of York – used these to add to their own collections.

Today, academic and institutional libraries make many of their purchases of rare or old books from sellers' catalogues. Browsing these, from a range of sellers, will give a good sense of the types of book out there to be bought, and prices for them.

Library catalogues and other lists

Catalogues of book collections date back to antiquity, and function as bibliographies, offering an overview of what had been written in a particular place by a particular time. They could be used as a wish list for people who liked (and could afford) books. And this is what happened with the earliest printed catalogues of European university libraries: Leiden University Library and the Bodleian Library were the first to issue these, in 1595 and 1605 respectively. The catalogues were used by scholars, private collectors and educational institutions as guides to building a collection. They provided examples of books to include in a library, and could even be used as the basis for one's own catalogue: several Oxford colleges wrote the shelf marks of their own collections beside the relevant books in the Leiden or Bodleian catalogues, as did the philosopher John Locke in his copy of the Bodleian 1674 catalogue.

Alongside these, another, more controversial, list of books was likely used by collectors in selecting what to buy: the Inquisition's various Indexes of authors or books to be banned or censored. These were first published in 1559, and updates were issued right up until 1961. The lists banned some authors and works in their entirety, and allowed others to be read provided they had certain passages crossed out. The lists have, at various points, banned works by the classical poet Lucretius, the medieval writer of English history Geoffrey of Monmouth, and poets, scientists and philosophers including Dante, Petrarch, Boccaccio, Galileo, Milton, Descartes, Newton and Darwin. There is speculation that the list in some cases had the opposite effect from the one intended, and aroused curiosity for some of these authors and their works.

Buying online

viaLibri claims to be the world's largest search engine for old, rare and second-hand books. It currently searches 147 sites, and is specifically recommended by the Provincial Book Fair Association. I tested it with a slight volume of poetry by Pat Galligan, an airman who was shot down over Cologne in 1943, and was offered two copies for sale. For comparison, there are no current listings for this book on eBay or BookFinder. I've tended to rely on AbeBooks for my own purchasing, but will also check viaLibri from now on if I already know the specific book I am looking for. If you enjoy browsing online, AbeBooks and online auction sites such as eBay offer hours of fun.

There are things to be aware of when buying online though, including scale, condition and authenticity. Is the book complete? It is quite common for pages to be missing, especially illustrations such as plates or maps, and this can be hard to check for online. Every page of every second-hand or antiquarian book that the Bodleian buys is counted to check it is complete.

Is the book advertised definitely the edition you want? Read the description carefully and check for the date and publisher of the copy on offer, as the original details are often given in descriptions of books that turn out to be modern on-demand (sometimes unofficial) reprints. Some of the images used to advertise books are stock photos and do not match the actual copy on sale. Check all these things before you buy, and you might want to ask for a photo, ideally with scale. Familiarize yourself with some key bookselling terms, to make sure you understand what you are getting. John Carter's *ABC for Book Collectors* is the standard guide, first published in 1952, but now revised and on its 9th edition (Oak Knoll Press, 2016). There is also a good free online dictionary of terms by Etherington and Roberts (see Appendix for details) covering much of the same ground. Both include explanations of abbreviations such as 'aeg' 'als' ('all edges gilt' and 'autograph letter signed'). You might need to know what a 'perfected' copy is (more on this below), or why a description includes the word 'genuine'. This last one always rings alarm bells with me, as it might if you were offered a 'genuine' Rolex. If you are spending more than a few pounds, make sure you read the terms of sale, and can send back any book that arrives and is not as described.

If you are buying books from abroad, keep abreast of any import or export rules from the country of sale as well as your own. For example, Italy does not allow the export of any book printed before 1965 without an export licence, so buying an old book online from overseas or while on holiday abroad could involve more expense than the purchase price and a great deal of hassle.

Book crooks

Where there's money to be made, illegal activity seems to follow, and the world of books is no exception. Opportunist thieves, scholars and even, alas, librarians have abused their positions to take financial advantage from collections to which they have access. The roll call of rogues is sadly long. It stretches from the ancient world, where Ashurbanipal, king of Assyria in the seventh century BCE, used a book curse to warn thieves away from tablets in the library of Nineveh, to the pilfering of the library of John Dee – mathematician and correspondent of angels – while he travelled abroad in the 1580s, right up to the present day, and the 'Mission Impossible' case in 2017 when thieves descended through the roof of a warehouse in Feltham and stole books in transit to a book fair. The theft and mutilation of books by those whose job it is to protect them seem perhaps the most pernicious. Cases that have come to light in the last decade or so include a caretaker at Lambeth Palace Library and the director of the Girolamini Library in Naples. Not only did they steal books, but they mutilated them to remove – or add – signs of ownership, ruining the individual books and diminishing our understanding of the whole collection of which they were a part. Buying from a reputable bookseller limits your chances of encountering a stolen book, though one of the most notorious thieves was himself a seller. Guglielmo Libri, an Italian who fled to France in 1831, then to England, to avoid a ten-year jail sentence with hard labour for his book thefts from libraries around Europe, sold many of his books at auctions in London. His pilfered treasures included a Leonardo da Vinci manuscript on the flight of birds.

Look out for inked library stamps in any book you are buying, and try to identify the library if you can (try an internet search for any text you can read on the stamp, or an image-matching search). If the library still exists, and there is no second stamp suggesting the book has been deaccessioned or released from the collection, get in touch with the library and ask whether they are missing that book. Look out, too, for attempts to erase marks of ownership such as inscriptions or bookplates: these will be cut away, crossed out, scratched from the paper or bleached, but often leave traces. While these are not necessarily signs of theft, as there was a vogue for removing past signs of use in books especially in the eighteenth and nineteenth centuries, library stamps are sometimes also removed in these ways.

In the UK, if you buy stolen property – even unwittingly – title (that is, ownership) of that item does not pass to you, but remains with the original owner, and could be forfeited. This will be different in other countries, so check your own rules, especially if you are spending a significant sum of money. Some recent book thieves have attempted to evade laws by auctioning stolen books in countries where title passes on sale (unlike the UK). The thieving director of the Girolamini Library mentioned above sold many stolen volumes via a German auction house Zisska & Schauer (both he and the seller were sent to prison), and the German auction house Ketterer Kunst received and sold on books stolen by a member of staff from the National Library of Sweden over a period of nearly twenty years. There are both national and international bodies that keep registers of missing or stolen books: ILAB; Lost Art, which records Nazi loot; a not-for-profit organization Artive; the private pay-per-search Art Loss Register; and even Interpol, though the focus of most of these bodies (except ILAB) is on works of art rather than books. As mentioned above, professional booksellers' associations have codes of conduct relating to theft, and will offer buyers a certain amount of confidence in what they are purchasing.

Fakes and forgeries

Guglielmo Libri not only stole books; he also meddled with them, adding fake inscriptions of notable historical figures; so too did the Girolamini Library thief, adding faked drawings to an edition of Galileo's *Sidereus nuncius* that were supposedly in Galileo's hand. Along with forged inscriptions and ownership marks, bindings can also be altered or faked. Nineteenth-century collectors were so keen to own Renaissance bookbindings that a thriving market of fakes was created. Giovanni Battista Grimaldi, a Genoese banker in the sixteenth century, had his books bound with a medallion of Apollo and Pegasus on the covers. In the

nineteenth and twentieth centuries forgers added copies
of this medallion to plain sixteenth-century bindings
as well as crafting entirely new bindings to pass off as
originals. In 1897 Sotheby, Wilkinson & Hodge issued
a sale catalogue with the title *Catalogue of a Remarkable
Collection of Books in Magnificent Modern Bindings,
Formed by an Amateur.* If you didn't spot the 'modern'
in the title, this would appear to be an extraordinary
collection of sixteenth-century bindings owned by
all the great book collectors of that century, from
French kings to Jean Grolier, to Diane de Poitiers.
Individual descriptions in this catalogue only mention
in a handful of cases that these are all forgeries by
Louis Hagué, sold to an unsuspecting English buyer
named John Blacker. He spent around £36,000 on
them, realized eventually what they were, and died.
His collection was sold after his death for just £1,907.
Earlier bindings were also targeted. A Sienese painter
and restorer named Icilio Joni forged painted wooden
bindings from the fourteenth century known as
biccherne that covered volumes of accounts in the State
Archive in his home city. He died in 1946; his forgeries
have since become valuable and collectible for their
own sake, selling for several thousand pounds. There is

one currently on display in the Treasures gallery at the British Library.

Pirated editions produced historically, to get around censorship or a lack of printing privilege, claim a false date, place of printing and sometimes even printer. There were also facsimile editions produced in the nineteenth century of much earlier printed materials, reproduced with the original date of printing. While most of these were not intended to trick buyers, they could mislead the unwary modern buyer taken in by the date on show.

I've heard distinguished and experienced collectors give their own accounts of falling prey to books that claimed to be something they were not. It is unlikely that you will become a victim here, unless spending large amounts of money. But there are some things to consider that can be less easy to spot. If you are buying older books, say printed before 1820, you might encounter 'perfected' copies. This is when a book that is missing some of its pages (properly, leaves), for whatever reason, has these leaves supplied from another copy, or in facsimile of some sort, and we can all be caught out here. Some forgers go to great lengths to recreate leaves that are almost indistinguishable from the originals; they even source paper from the right period on which to print their fake pages. If you are spending a reasonable sum, you might enlist the help of a reputable bookseller, a book consultant or a friendly rare-books librarian or book conservator, for a second opinion.

Price

How do you know whether the price being asked for a book is fair? There is no simple and straightforward answer to this, especially if you are out and about in a bookshop and are considering a spur-of-the-moment purchase. I would be tempted to say that if you like it and can afford it, it's a fair price. But be aware that some booksellers do charge more for a particular book than others, even when condition is roughly comparable; they might have a wealthier client base, and be in a fancy neighbourhood with high overheads.

If you are buying online, or have some time to dig about before committing to a purchase, you could look for a comparable copy for sale online: you will need to find the same edition, ideally in the same sort of condition (bearing in mind the difference that binding can make to a price). If you are looking at an online listing, remember that this is an asking price, and not actually what the book is worth. You might also search for auction results, which will confirm prices that have been paid for the book. If you can't find any other copies sold or for sale, have a look at library catalogues such as JISC Library Hub Discover or WorldCat to see how many copies you can see in libraries around the world. This will give you a sense of its rarity.

As we saw above in the case of the edition of Byron that I purchased for £10, prices for the same edition vary wildly. The most expensive copy on sale, at £1,556, is described as being in 'excellent' condition. Another seller is offering the same edition in 'very good' condition for £504, with Queen Adelaide as one of its former owners. As you can see, the prices being asked for a good copy of this book vary considerably, and suggest the difficulty in knowing whether a price being asked is a good one. The more you peruse book fairs and catalogues, the stronger your instinct will become for whether a price is fair.

Condition

As we've seen with some of the examples above, condition is often key to the price of a book. When buying a book for anything more than a few pounds, before you purchase it look through it carefully for torn, missing or loose leaves (see if all the page numbers follow in sequence), and for signs of damage from water, mould, insects or rodents. Chapter 5 sets out some common problems that afflict books and what can and cannot be done about them. When you are considering a purchase, ask yourself whether the problems can be fixed; whether you can live with the condition or imperfection; and whether the book will present you with problems in the future. If you are buying more expensive books as an investment, condition will be key to their resale value.

Shelving and Storing Books

> There's a shop opposite Caesar's forum ... look for me there; ... out of the first or second pigeon-hole he will give you Martial, smoothed with pumice, and elegant in purple.
>
> Martial, *Epigrams* 1.117

How do you house your books? Well, aside from the piles on the floor to which we are turning a blind eye, the obvious answer is – on shelves. But habits have changed over time. Books haven't always been books as we think of them now, and they've been stored and displayed in or on things other than shelves. When we think of a 'book', we almost certainly think of a codex – that is, a sequence of leaves held together along one edge to turn over as we read. But texts have been written on a variety of surfaces for thousands of years, and the codex is a relative newcomer; it is linked to the growth of Christianity in the first and second centuries CE. Storage systems for books have changed accordingly, from pigeonholes and niches for the papyrus rolls, such as that described above by Martial, to the cupboards and chests used for books in the Middle Ages, the presses with sloping desks and rods to chain books in the early modern period, and shelves and bookcases as we know them now.

Even though most of our books these days are in codex form and the majority have roughly similar dimensions, if you need shelves for your books there are still many options depending on your space, your budget and how visible you want your books to be. Should you have fixed, adjustable or even moving shelving? Should your shelves or cases have doors? Of what should they be made?

Book cupboards and cases

Book cupboards were designed for codices, but could house rolls too if needed, and were used in late antiquity and the Middle Ages. In the first century CE Pliny the Younger had one in his bedroom, set into the wall, for books that were to be read and reread. There are some early illustrations showing these in a range of sizes. The seventh-century manuscript known as the Codex Amiatinus illustrates one with five shelves, the books all lying flat with their spines facing out; another, with three shelves for books, is depicted on the wall of the chapel encompassing the tomb of Empress Galla Placidia of Ravenna, commissioned by her between about 425 and 450 CE. There are much larger ones later on, such as the book cupboards in the Vatican Library that span 7 feet in height and 2 feet in depth (work started on the library in 1587), and the incredible painted ones that line the walls of the library of St Mary's church in the parish of Langley Marish in Berkshire, from the seventeenth century.

According to Sid G. Hedges in *The Universal Book of Hobbies and Handicrafts* (first published 1936), the first thing to decide when it comes to bookcases is whether to have glass fronted or open ones. The diarist Samuel Pepys is thought to have been one of the first to own glass-fronted bookcases, and you can see them at Magdalene College, Cambridge. Book cupboards or cases with doors will help to keep dust off your books, but will inhibit air circulation, and leave them at risk of mould, as Chapter 4 explains in more detail.

Free-standing cases are a great option if you want to buy second-hand or, like me, you are hopeless with drilling into walls. Depending on how stable it is and how high, you might still need to fix the top of the case to the wall with a safety bracket, though, to stop it falling on anyone. One downside of free-standing bookcases is that they might not make the most of the space you have in your room, and in many cases the shelves themselves are not adjustable and limit further what you can put in them.

Flexible shelving

If you want shelving to fit your space more precisely, there are many options for different budgets and differing skills in DIY. Sid Hedges, from whom we heard above, mentions an easy and screw-free way of rustling some up: if you have access to bricks, and some planks of wood such as old floorboards, you can assemble a basic set of low shelves. My parents built shelves of this sort when we were growing up, alongside more sophisticated sets (bookcases, really) all of wood, with sides and compartments.

If you have planks but no bricks, and prefer something sturdier that can be more easily adjusted, vertical metal wall fixings with brackets to hold the planks in place are a good option. Our house had a whole room with home-made shelves of this sort when we moved in, and they held vast numbers of books. Over the years we've taken half of them out to turn the room into a bedroom, and screwed the remainder into their bracket so that they don't tip their contents onto small children. They've been remarkably durable, and solid pine shelves of this sort can take a lot of weight without sagging: we've tested them with endless hardback annuals and volumes of the *Guinness Book of Records* and *Asterix*. The more modern MDF ones we put up elsewhere all quickly bowed under the weight of our adult equivalents of these bigger books.

Single shelves

Don't underestimate the usefulness of a single shelf. You could put one up with wall brackets just below the ceiling around an entire room, giving ample space for paperbacks or light books without any loss of floor or living space. We have these in two small bedrooms, currently filled with soft animal toys, but one day, perhaps, they will more helpfully house paperback novels.

Shelves made to measure

Custom-built options could include a shelving system for your entire house, or even just a single bookcase, if you have a large group of similar-sized books, or know exactly what you want on it. This could be from a traditional joinery or ordered online. I have a narrow pine one (120 × 180 × 15 cm) with ten compartments, made fifteen years ago at a joinery for £200. Do build compartments into your design rather than a single unbroken shelf, as this helps to keep books upright and in manageable groups when you take books out to read. Ours was a simple design, conceived specifically to house Penguin paperbacks. More elaborate custom-made bookcases for different sizes of book will cost a great deal more than this. You could really go to town here. One of the most impressive sets of shelves I've seen is at the Wormsley Library, owned by the Getty family. Their lovely wooden cases each have a retractable surface that pulls out like a drawer at waist height for you to rest any book on that you want to have open in front of you.

Rolling shelves

If you have more books than you can store around the walls of your rooms, and have a spare room or basement or garage, you could borrow a leaf from institutional libraries and install rolling stacks. These are bookcases on tracks on the floor that can be moved just enough to allow access to one aisle at a time; they cram a lot into a small space, roughly double (some companies claim three times) as many books as regular shelves. While these are for storage rather than for show, they do allow easier access to books than storage boxes. The British Museum, which housed the collections that then became the British Library, had rolling shelves installed in the 1880s, suspended from ceiling girders. William Gladstone, when he wasn't being prime minister, developed this idea further with his plan for wheeled bookshelves in the Bodleian that rolled sideways into a shared aisle instead of forwards, and these were fitted into a new basement under Radcliffe Square in the early twentieth century. The Bodleian Library uses modern rolling shelving for its stacks in central Oxford, though the majority of its books are now stored off-site in a warehouse at Swindon in trays on fixed shelving that stretches 11 metres high, fetched by staff on motorized cherry pickers. If you are thinking of shelving very many books in a small space, do remember that they can weigh rather a lot. In some storage areas of the Bodleian's Weston Library the load is 1 ton per square metre.

Book racks and troughs

> Walker's adjustable book rack … will hold upright any size of book … for the study, for the library, for the drawing room.
>
> The Art and Stationery Company advertisement, Oxford, 1895

I only discovered these a few years ago, from frequenting my local antiques market, but I love a book rack. Made of wood, sometimes extendable, and with ends that fold up and down, these little single shelves are ideal for smaller books (in spite of the advert above) and can be displayed on a desk or on top of other furniture. I've found nice oak ones from the early twentieth century that I've given as presents, and a very small mahogany one with inlays that I've kept for myself that is perfect for the small Italian leather-bound notebooks that I can't stop myself from buying.

Book troughs are similar, but without folding or extendable parts, and are good for a small group of

pocket editions, such as the *Observer's Books* published
by Frederick Warne & Co. in the middle decades of the
twentieth century.

Revolving bookcases

You will know these, of course, from bookshops and
libraries, but you can also get nice wooden ones for use
at home. Many companies offer them online, and a tall
slim one would be a good space-saving option for the
corner of a room or landing. Again, if you are feeling
flush there are some wonderful antique ones made of
woods such as mahogany and satinwood, and many are
on castors and can be moved around.

Unusual bookcases

It's quite fun searching online for antique bookcases,
as there are some I'd never thought of, such as the
double-sided 'waterfall' bookcase on wheels. It's a bit like
a more elegant version of a library trolley, with shelves
cascading down each side. Another lovely example at the
Victoria and Albert Museum is a bookcase with folding
desk made in Lima in the late eighteenth century that
is inlaid all over with mother of pearl. You can find
circular bookcases either to fit a curved wall or as a

stand-alone feature, and sculptural shelves such as green metal ones from the 1980s, or a contemporary marble block with tin shelves jutting out from them. Perhaps best of all is the wonderful Penguin Donkey designed by Egon Riss in the 1930s for the Isokon Furniture Company. This wooden donkey-shaped shelving unit was designed for the new Penguin paperbacks, and also had a space in the centre for newspapers or magazines. It remains popular to this day, and is still produced by Isokon, now in a range of colours.

Materials

What are shelves made from, and what should you use for yours? The library at Nineveh is thought to have had slate shelves, though wood has now been the preferred material for many centuries, joined by metal shelving in the late nineteenth century (powder-coated metal has now replaced cast iron). The main risk of metal is rust, and the main risk of wood is susceptibility to pests. If you go for wood rather than metal, solid wood is much stronger and less likely to sag than MDF, and soft woods such as pine will do. Conservators would be worried about risks to collections both from unsealed wood and from coatings or varnishes on the wood, as these can release volatile organic compounds (VOCs) that could harm books. This is probably not something to worry about in your home, though you should leave any polished, varnished or treated wooden shelves to air for as long as you can before filling them, and you could line them with acid-free card to protect against some of these pollutants. There are many ranges of varnishes available now that are water-based and without VOCs.

If you are cleaning your shelves, I would suggest simply using a damp (not wet) cloth. If you must use cleaning products, make sure they are thoroughly wiped away, and the shelves completely dry before replacing any books. If you want to polish wooden shelves, a small amount of beeswax, buffed thoroughly, might do. I'm not sure about the 'Argonaut', a combined wood varnish and stain on sale in the late nineteenth century, which promised to be 'hard and durable and perfectly free from stickiness'.

Reaching your shelves

There is a wonderful photo of Nigella Lawson sitting in her library against a backdrop of shelves that stretch several metres up to the ceiling. Many of the books are on a lean, which is a bit distracting, but my main worry is how she reaches them. There is no elegant step ladder in sight, and in any case it would need to be enormous to reach to the top. She would need the sort of ladder that used to slide along a rail on the walls of the room that housed the colourful boxes of printed ephemera that formed the John Johnson Collection at the Bodleian. The Bodleian also used to have lovely sets of wooden steps with a vertical pole at the top to hold on to while reaching for a book, which you can still see in some stately homes. These were banished some years ago, alas, and replaced with huge metal frames on wheels that disappear to form a secure base when you start climbing. You will no doubt prefer to house the former, and for extra versatility you can find versions that fold into a library chair.

Placing books on shelves

Even when books are on shelves, rather than in boxes or cupboards, they haven't always been placed as we think of them now. Sometimes they were shelved horizontally rather than vertically, and their spines did not always face out. The textblock edge (that is, the leaf edges on the three sides of the book that are not the spine) was often on view, either the fore-edge or the upper or lower edge, often with a handwritten title so that books could be identified. It was easier to write titles on the paper edges of the textblock than on a shiny or dark leather spine; it was only in the eighteenth century that spine labels – extra pieces of leather tooled with the title, or paper ones handwritten – became common on books. In some cases the textblock edges were elaborately decorated with tooling and gilding, and even paintings. One of the most famous examples of this is the library that belonged to the Pillone family in Italy. In the sixteenth century the family had portraits of the authors painted onto the fore-edges of their books.

These days, books come in publishers' bindings with titles on the spine, to be shelved with the spines facing outwards. So, unless your collection is very old, or you are very eccentric or have the skill to add your own fore-edge paintings or titles, let's assume that you will shelve yours spine out.

But should your books be placed as far back on the shelves as possible, to keep dust away, and maximize storage for knick-knacks, or at the front, or somewhere in between? You will be able to handle them most easily and safely if they are kept towards the front. The gentlest way to remove a book from a shelf is not to grab it by the top of the spine and pull, but to push the two books either side of it a centimetre or two away from the shelf edge, leaving the book you want with enough spine exposed for you to hold it on either side, and slide it from the shelf. This works for CDs too, as long as they are not packed too tightly, and in both cases saves on the amount of room you need at the top of each shelf: just enough for air to circulate, rather than worrying about whether you need finger space to manoeuvre books out. And books should not be packed too tightly onto a shelf, as some covers might stick together, or catch against one another (for example, anything with metal clasps or bosses).

Larger books, say anything over about 40 cm, should be kept flat (unless a very slight volume) to ease pressure from the weight of the textblock on the binding. If you are planning a new bookshelf, include several spaces of perhaps 10–15 cm in height, each capable of housing two or three large books lying down on their side with spine facing out. You don't want a huge stack of these on a shelf of normal height, as it will be impossible to get to those at the bottom.

Leaving space for growth

Leaving space on your shelves for new books is difficult, and might seem extravagant. But if you have your books in a particular order, and are adding to your collection, keep some space at the end of each shelf. You can fill it temporarily with a book on a stand with its cover on display, or an ornament, until you need the space. Use bookends to hold the books on an unfilled shelf in place. An enormous variety of these are available, in about any design you can imagine, often highly decorative and taking up lots of space. My favourites are the thin plain metal ones with a foot that slips under the last few books on the shelf. Years of wrestling with rows of heavy children's books and trying to hold them in place with chunky wooden Mr Men bookends have convinced me that nothing beats a slim L-shaped metal one.

Security

Richard de Bury advises keeping your precious books higher up, out of reach of hands and eyes, and seven hundred years later this is still good advice. The Bodleian Library chained all but its smallest books in the seventeenth and eighteenth centuries, so that they wouldn't wander. Chaining very small books is fiddly and impractical (though some libraries did it), and they were usually kept on the highest shelves where only staff could fetch them, or in lockable cupboards, sometimes with metal grilles or trelliswork so that the books were still visible. You can see many remaining examples in stately homes open to the public, and at the magnificent Morgan Library in New York City.

Display cases

Most of us don't have room for display cases in our homes, let alone one especially for books. But do consider showing some of your books off, either at the end of a shelf, or alongside other treasures of pottery, teddy bears or glass ornaments. Small folding stands for displaying plates will work for some books and let you show off interesting covers.

Moving books around

Buckets were used to carry rolls to and from their shelves or niches in the ancient world; chests or book boxes were used in the Middle Ages to move books from one dwelling to another; and barrels were used commercially and for the removal of large collections of books. Some small collections, put together with travel in mind, even had their own custom-made boxes. William Hakewill, a lawyer and politician, presented sets of small uniformly bound books as gifts in the early seventeenth century, each set in a single book-shaped box that opened to reveal three shelves. These were portable, and allowed the recipient to have a selection of classic works to hand. Napoleon and Roosevelt also had their own travelling libraries of small matching books in a box; the latter had his bound in a robust pigskin and took them on safari.

These days you will most likely use cardboard boxes or plastic crates for moving books. Small boxes are best in both cases, so that they remain manageable to lift and handle, and lids will keep the books clean, protect them from damage and allow the boxes to be stacked. When libraries move books from one location to another, they use plastic crates with books placed upright in the crate, as though on a shelf, and filled so that the single row of books is held securely in place, with wedges of foam filling up any extra space. This is generally a better way to move books than to have one piled on top of another and sliding round in a box with the corners getting bumped, though large or heavy books will need to be stacked horizontally. Use packing paper, bits of foam salvaged from other packaging, or even old clothes or small blankets to pad out extra space in boxes that are to be transported. Check regularly any boxes you have in storage for signs of pests.

Sending books

Booksellers and library donors use a variety of materials to package their books for bringing or sending into a library. As someone who often unwraps these parcels or bundles, I have firm favourites. Ideally, a book should be wrapped first in plain paper that will not run or seep into the book should it encounter any moisture. White tissue paper or plain packing paper is best, much though I love the orange and purple tissue papers and hand-marbled papers that sometimes arrive in the post. Paper tape such as masking tape should be used to keep the paper in place, rather than sticky tape, and certainly not parcel tape. A layer or two of bubble wrap (depending on the size of the book) offers protection against bumping. This can then go in a jiffy bag or simply be wrapped up in parcel paper. At this point, most people use parcel tape to seal up the parcel paper, and that is OK, as you are now far away from the actual book itself. If you are sending a book that is valuable, send it by recorded delivery, insured for the correct amount (usually at a cost of just a few pounds).

Travelling with books

You are unlikely to be travelling with book boxes, book chests or a custom-made travelling library (congratulations if you are!), but other old ways of protecting books might still be useful.

Some books had a protective secondary cover of leather or textile that could be wrapped around the book to protect it; this was common with girdle books, which hung at the waist on a chain; others had their own *chemises*, essentially little fabric bags to protect delicate bindings such as textile or embroidered ones. If you are travelling, you might consider wrapping your books up in your clothes to keep the corners from bending. Or, if you regularly have a book in your bag, you might want a book pouch to keep it from scuffing.

Conditions for Books

[Position your library] within some spacious Court, or Garden, where it may enjoy a free light, a good and agreeable prospect; the air pure, not near to marshes, sinks or dung-hills ... the West winds are more troublesom and noxious, and the Meridional more dangerous than all the rest, for that being hot and moist they dispose things to corruption, thicken the air, nourish wormes, engender vermine, foment and create sicknesses, disposing us to new ones.

Gabriel Naudé, *Advis pour dresser une bibliothèque*, in John Evelyn's translation of 1661

MOST OF US are stuck with the atmospheric conditions that we have in our homes. This chapter suggests some steps to take to keep your books in the best possible condition for your circumstances.

It lists some common hazards, and why and how to avoid them, and offers advice on how to treat minor mishaps that might befall your books. You should seek advice from a professional conservator if you have active mould, or books damaged by fire or floodwater. The Institute of Conservation (Icon) in the UK keeps a register of professional conservators, and will help you to find one.

Temperature and humidity

A stable environment with minimal fluctuations in temperature and relative humidity is best for books. When Gabriel Naudé wrote his book of advice on setting up a library in the 1620s, he suggested placing it on a middle floor. There it would evade dampness from the ground that leads to mould, as well as the wildly fluctuating temperatures of attics. This is why many medieval and early modern libraries are built on the first floor, for example Duke Humfrey's Library, the oldest purpose-built part of what is now the Bodleian Library. Icon recommends storing books at a temperature of 16–19°c, with relative humidity at 45–60 per cent. When the Bodleian lends books for exhibitions, it asks for a stable environment: the temperature can be 18–24°c, but must not vary by more or less than 3 degrees in a given 24-hour period; the relative humidity must be 45–55 per cent, but again must not go up or down by more than 5 per cent within the same period. These are the sorts of standards used by specialist libraries and museums responsible for preserving cultural heritage. The temperature and relative humidity in your home will vary throughout the year, unless you have a special stable environment that can be controlled, such as the compartments in which the Bodleian stores its books. Outside of these recommended ranges there is a greater risk of damage to your books from mould and pests, and from materials becoming brittle. Obviously we can only control these to some degree, but different rooms will have different conditions, and you might house your books accordingly. You can buy a cheap electronic temperature and relative humidity monitor to work out which area of your home is most suitable for your books.

If the relative humidity is too low, and the air too dry, certain materials used in the production of books, including paper and leather, can shrink and crack. Too much moisture – that is, a high relative humidity – will tempt mould and insects to set up home. A high relative humidity is also linked to corrosion of metal, such as staples used in some kinds of smaller publications, or nails used in the bindings of books from the sixteenth century or earlier.

If your home is too dry, you could add pot plants or simple ceramic humidifiers that hang on radiators. If too moist, you could remove some of this with a plug-in electric dehumidifier; improve ventilation with an extractor fan or by opening a window; or use a desiccant for small spaces, such as the packets of silica that come in packaging for everything from shoes to Covid lateral-flow tests.

Generally, as long as your books are not in a kitchen, bath or shower room, in a damp basement, a hot dry attic, or above a radiator or fireplace, you will be avoiding the worst places. If possible, books should be shelved against an internal not external wall, again to avoid damp and fluctuating temperatures.

Mould

> a small white spot of hairy mould, multitudes of which I found to bespeck & whiten over the red covers of a small book ... These spots appear'd, through a good microscope, to be a very pretty shap'd vegetative body, which, from almost the same part of the leather, shot out multitudes of small long cylindrical and

transparent stalks, not exactly streight, but a little
bended with the weight of a round and white knob
that grew on the top of each of them ... The whole
substance of these pretty bodies was of a very tender
constitution, much like the substance of a softer kind
of common white mushroms.

> Robert Hooke, *Micrographia*, 1665

This is how Robert Hooke, one of the discoverers of microorganisms, described them for the first time in print. He illustrated this micro-fungus growing on a book with a wonderful engraving based on observations through his microscope.

Mould grows from spores that are all around us, and will do so when the conditions are right. When relative humidity reaches 65 per cent there is a real risk of mould in dark places with a lack of circulating air, on materials used for book-making such as paper, leather and wood, and on any accumulated dust or dirt. Mould produces enzymes that dissolve these organic materials and pose an irreversible threat to your books.

Mould is also potentially dangerous to human health, and should be treated with caution. General advice on handling mouldy items is to wear vinyl or nitrile gloves, an FFP2 or FFP3 mask, and goggles. Dry and inactive mould can be wiped off in a well-ventilated area, but active mould that is damp and smears when rubbed needs to be quickly dried out, and should be treated by a professional conservator. You should freeze any mouldy books in a sealed plastic bag until they can be treated professionally (see below for freezing).

  I keep music scores in an old piano stool in a ground-floor room that is considerably colder than the rest of the house. It has poor air circulation, and mould periodically grows on them. This also happens to books in cupboards in colder rooms, as they do need ventilation. Make sure that any cupboards you use for books have some means of ventilation: this could be as simple as drilling a series of holes on each side to allow air in, or even leaving the doors open regularly. Keep an eye on books in any such places so that you can spot mould early. While a 70:30 solution of ethanol and water will kill mould, and some people recommend this for treating it, the ethanol can react with other substances, and is not recommended for use on books or paper. I wipe it off with a cloth in a well-ventilated area (outdoors if possible).

Water

> You will perhaps see a stiff-necked youth, lounging sluggishly in his study: while the frost pinches him in winter time, oppressed with cold, his watery nose drops, nor does he take the trouble to wipe it with his handkerchief till it has moistened the book beneath it with its vile dew … and while he adduces a multitude of reasons void of physical meaning, he waters the book, spread out upon his lap, with the sputtering of his saliva.
>
> Richard de Bury, *Philobiblon*, 1345, translated by J.B. Inglis, 1832

I'm sure you treat your books with more care. But do consider where they are stored in relation to other sources of water. Keep them away from window ledges where the windows have a tendency to become fogged up with condensation; and from sinks, and possible sources of leaks including overhead pipes.

Your books will probably not suffer as dramatic a fate as those of the antiquary and bishop Thomas Tanner. His collection of nearly 1,000 volumes was transported to Oxford from Norwich in 1731, and fell from its barge into the water along the way. According to old accounts, the books were submerged for twenty hours before most were recovered. Some rarities did not survive, but among those that did was a copy of a book that is now the most expensive printed book ever to sell at auction: the book of Psalms printed in Harvard, Massachusetts, in 1640, known as the 'Bay Psalm Book'. Only eleven copies survive, and one was sold for $14 million in 2013. The Bodleian copy escaped without too much damage, though it – and almost all the other books in the collection – had to be rebound in the nineteenth century.

If one of your books falls into the bath (perhaps you've forgotten to use your Floating Book Caddy for Bath, Pool and Hot Tub, or your You-bumi Waterproof Book Cover, both created for the bathing book-lover), or meets a similar fate to those of Tanner, you need to act promptly, to stop mould from growing: growth can start within forty-eight hours. If you don't have time to dry your book, you can freeze it for a later time. The advice that follows is for books damaged by clean or fresh water. If you have been flooded, and there is a danger of contaminated water such as sewage, take expert advice from a professional conservator.

Let's gloss over this advice from Timotheo Rossello from 1559:

> Take the leg bones of a calf or heifer cooked in the fire and reduced to a powder, and grind it up with a bit of fresh water; put it on the book where it is wet, and it will suck it dry perfectly, without any damage.
> Rossello, *Della summa de' secreti*, 1559

HOW TO FREEZE (TO DRY AT A LATER TIME)

Wrap your wet book in white or uncoloured paper towels, then seal it in a plastic bag and place it in your domestic freezer. When you are ready to dry your book, remove it from the freezer and let it come up to room temperature in the plastic bag. Check it frequently, and remove the wrapping as soon as it reaches room temperature.

HOW TO DRY OUT WET BOOKS

Place your book upright on a dry surface on an old light-coloured towel, tea towel or uncoloured paper towels; if the surface is wooden, cover it with plastic first. It should be in a room with low relative humidity and good air circulation, such as a breeze from outside, or near a gentle fan blowing cold (not hot) air. If the book is sodden, don't try to open it, simply let it stand closed until it stops dripping. Then gently fan the pages out to an angle of up to 60 degrees, with the book still upright. If you are using a fan to move air, it should not ruffle the pages. Do not put your book in a low oven, over a heater, next to a fire or in a microwave, as you might melt its adhesives, warp the book or singe the pages.

Leave your book like this until it is thoroughly dry. If you are drying a pamphlet, you can hang it over a washing line to dry out fully (make sure the line is clean); printers hang up their printed sheets to dry in this way. If you have any leaves that are stuck together, try to ease them apart gently. You could use a bone folder, which looks like a rounded blunt letter opener made of a flat smooth piece of bone, for this kind of delicate turning of pages (they are used especially by bookbinders), or you could substitute an old-fashioned blunt and rounded table knife.

Once the book is completely dry, you might find that the leaves have buckled and warped. To flatten these out, place the book underneath a heavy book or two (depending on the size, and how delicate it is) for a week or more. If your book is an antiquarian one, or not especially robust, you might prefer to squeeze it between other books on a (temporarily) tightly packed shelf rather than putting it beneath something heavy.

Light

All light will fade your books over time. Libraries, museums and stately homes closely monitor amounts of light reaching their collection items, especially those on exhibition. Light damage is cumulative, and can happen fairly quickly. We are all familiar with lux levels when buying light bulbs, and this same unit applies to exposure to visible light. Ultraviolet light, measured in microwatts per lumen, is also damaging to books. Lighting for exhibitions at the Bodleian is kept below 50 lux and 75 lumen. What does this mean for your books at home? Some smartphones have lux meters on them, and you can also purchase hand-held devices, to see what conditions you have (though these will change dramatically throughout the year). But knowing what light exposure you have won't help to determine which colours on which books will be most likely to fade, or fade quickest, as different inks and dyes fade at different rates. It is best to take a few simple steps to minimize damage.

House your books out of direct sunlight and away from bright windows, especially those that face south. If this is impossible, and you don't want your books to fade or the top edge of the textblock to darken, use blinds, net curtains, or line the inside of your windows with ultra-violet film, an adhesive plastic film that blocks UV rays, available from specialist suppliers. If you have the choice, you might like to keep your most precious books in a corridor without any windows. Our most treasured volumes at home are on shelves in a windowless corridor, including on a shelf that runs up the height of our stairwell. Do consider whether you have a dark stair or corridor space that could take shelves.

At home I have a modern series in paperback near a south-facing window; the rates at which the vibrant colours have faded on the spines is fascinating. Most have just turned a slightly lighter shade of their original colour, but the bright red volume has faded to white on the spine, and an orange one is now a very pale orange; in this case, red and orange appear to be much more vulnerable than the blues, greens and yellows used on the other covers. Cloth and leather bindings will also fade; in the case of leather, these generally become a drab brown, whatever lovely colour they once were.

If you leave a book open for a long time, some coloured inks used in printing will also fade, and some paper browns when overexposed to light. Institutions have in the past exhibited favourite books for decades, and this had led to a browning of the openings on display, and fading of those that are hand-coloured. The Bay Psalm book mentioned earlier was on display at the Bodleian for some thirty years, and now has a noticeably browned title page. Another is a much earlier book of psalms, written in gold ink on purple parchment in the ninth century; this beautiful book was also on display in the library for at least three decades, and some of the purple has faded. There are many other types of material that would fade quickly if exposed to light for more than brief periods: ink from felt-tip pens and biro can be particularly vulnerable, and fades quickly if left open to the light; watercolours and early photographs are also at risk. Our collections at home are unlikely to have their pages open to light, but, if they do, note that light damage is cumulative and cannot be reversed.

Dust

For any Philip Pullman fans, I don't mean souls and the invisible life force of the universe, but rather the visible and disappointingly recurring detritus that gathers on our books. I confess to having books that are sometimes dusty, and they really shouldn't be: over time dust builds up and will encourage pests and mould that feed on it and leave their mark.

If your books are robust, you might consider cleaning them with a vacuum. The hand-held sort used for cars or pet hair or a regular domestic one will be alright, as long as it has a soft brush attachment and a low suction setting. You can buy expensive custom-made conservation vacuums (and even entire book-dusting machines), but many libraries use a regular vacuum with a good filter and small soft nozzle. You could also attach a piece of fabric such as netting or cheesecloth over the suction end and secure it in place with a rubber band – this will prevent pieces of book being sucked up by accident. Run the nozzle gently in one direction over or just above the exposed edges, rather than back and forth. But if your books are fragile, and likely to lose any bits in the process, clean them instead by hand, with a soft brush such as an artist's paintbrush. Hold the book in one hand with your fingers on either side of the spine and brush dust off the top edge in gentle sweeping strokes away from the spine and from you. Dusters and cloths are abrasive and can catch on the books, so should be avoided, as should sponges and rubbers.

Shelves are reasonably good at keeping dust off books, so it is always better to keep books within shelves rather than on top of them. Some libraries attach flexible flaps (dustfalls), often with a scalloped edge, to the top of each shelf to further limit the amount of dust. Naudé thought this a practical and attractive solution. However, these can limit air circulation, and make access to the books more difficult; the British Library suggests that they should be avoided, and they are not used in the Bodleian. Dust does have a way of getting everywhere, even into cupboards, so the best option is to dust regularly. Some would say once a month, but realistically once a year would be good.

Pests

> Books heretofore most delicate, now become corrupted and abominable, lay lifeless, covered indeed with the excrements of mice and pierced through with the gnawing of worms; and those that were formerly clothed with purple and fine linen, were now seen reposing in dust and ashes, given over to oblivion, the abodes of moths.
>
> Richard de Bury, Philobiblon

This is how Richard de Bury described what he found in the cabinets and caskets of England's monasteries in the fourteenth century. Check your books regularly for signs of pests. You have probably seen second-hand or older books with small round holes on the covers or inside the textblock, passing through several leaves, or even leaving a long thin trail. These are made by what are popularly referred to as bookworms, 'the worst enemy of the Muses' (*Palatine Anthology*, 9.251), but are most likely the larvae of furniture beetles. These like wood, and sometimes make their way from wooden shelving and furniture into books, leaving holes as they eat their way through looking for an exit. If the holes are all empty, the damage is old; and any frass (i.e. larvae droppings) can be brushed gently away. Occasionally you might see a grub in one of the holes, in which case you should freeze the book for two weeks, sealed in a plastic bag. If you are tempted to buy a second-hand book with holes in it, seal it in a plastic bag before taking it home, and freeze it straight away, so as not to bring pests into your home.

Varied carpet beetle, biscuit beetle larvae, silverfish and woodlice will also eat damp paper and animal glues. If you see any active grubs or signs of insect activity, freeze the book as above, sealed in a plastic bag. You might also see tiny booklice; these are thought to feed on mould on books, but not damage the books themselves. Did you know that the library at the palace of Mafra in Portugal uses bats for pest control? Library staff cover up surfaces every night so that the bats that roost behind the shelves can gobble up insects, though of course they leave considerable mess of their own.

Rodents

Check your books for signs of rodent damage, too. Mice and rats will nibble books and loose papers if given a chance. A mouse greatly enjoyed a shoebox I had filled with letters, and one even found its way to a thirteenth-century reissue of the Magna Carta now kept in the Bodleian; the charter was stored folded when the mouse nibbled a hole in it that appears as three holes when the document is unfolded. Rats' nests found under floorboards at Oxburgh Hall in Norfolk proved a treasure trove of Tudor textiles, and also contained fragments of leaves from early printed books and a sixteenth-century music manuscript. If you find signs of damage or droppings on or near your books, you will need to have the rodents removed. You could try a humane trap, depending on the size of your problem and whether you have access to open countryside to release them into.

Inserts

> He goes out in the rain, and returns, and now flowers
> make their appearance upon our soil. Then the
> scholar we are describing, the neglecter rather than
> the inspecter of books, stuffs his volume with firstling
> violets, roses, and quadrifoils.
>
> Richard de Bury, Philobiblon

Many of us are guilty of using books as folders and storage vessels for souvenirs, photographs and special botanical finds. As a child, I doubted that four-leaf clovers really existed, as I'd looked so long and hard to find them. I was delighted when I bought an old edition of Homer's *Odyssey* at a village sale for a pound and found it to be full of them, pressed between the leaves of the book.

Some people like to fill their books with clippings and cuttings and articles that are directly or tangentially relevant. Where better to put a disposable map of Venice and a business card for a favourite restaurant than inside your copy of a guidebook to Venice? How else would you ever find them again? I have a friend who adds ephemeral souvenirs to any book he reads on holiday, so that it becomes filled with bits of memorabilia that record where and when he read it.

Alas all these things leave their mark, as they are often made of low-quality acidic paper (especially newspapers and magazines) and plastics (modern till receipts). One of the Bodleian's recently acquired collections of antiquarian books is full of these. Their owner was a doctor, and used the vast quantity of free stationery advertising drugs that came his way as bookmarks or to write his research and reference notes on. Many of his books contained several of these slips, printed on cheap paper that has gone brown over the decades and sometimes discoloured the pages it touches. Most of these have now been removed, to prevent further discolouration of his precious old books.

Newspaper and till receipts discolour particularly fast, and should not find a home in your books. If you do have a filing system of this sort, and can't bear to dismantle it, consider placing your cuttings in an archival polyester sleeve or wallet inside the front or back cover of the book (for supplies, see Appendix). The same applies to post-it notes and sticky plastic tabs. These leave a residue that will attract dirt and dust, and eventually cause damage. An elegant solution used in the past was to stick on permanent index tabs, usually of parchment or leather (I've seen a wonderful example with faces and acorns doodled over them), and sometimes intricately knotted cord ones. These were most often used on larger Bibles to mark the different books, although I saw one example recently of a small Bible from the mid-seventeenth century with perhaps a hundred or more tabs, so densely packed that any practical purpose was lost.

Food and drink

> He is not ashamed to eat fruit and cheese over an open book, and to transfer his empty cup from side to side upon it: and because he has not his alms-bag at hand, he leaves the rest of the fragments in his books.
> Richard de Bury, *Philobiblon*

Keep food and drink away from books, and avoid the wrath of Richard de Bury towards the careless scholar who eats and drinks over books, allowing crumbs to fall into the gutter, and the pages to be spoiled with grease.

Books – though often lying around in enticing fashion – are not coasters. You can probably buy book-shaped coasters if these make you happy, but don't use your books for this. Heat and moisture from even the most carefully handled vessel, sipped as neatly as though by Chaucer's prioress, will leave marks on the cover of a book, whether leather-bound or paperback. There are some examples in the Bodleian of dark rings on leather bindings made by hot things or by wine glasses.

Leather dressing and boot polish

If you have any leather-bound books, you might have considered using a dressing on them for protection or to bring out the grain. This used to be standard guidance for books in antiques guides, and is still practised by some booksellers and book owners. If you search the internet you will find a 'British Museum Leather Dressing' that is made of lanolin, cedar oil, beeswax and solvent, and my attention was recently drawn to this letter to Bodley's Librarian in 1950:

> Many thanks for the formula for leather dressing. Unfortunately no chemist here can make it up; bees wax and cedar-wood oil are not obtainable, and they don't know anything about hexane! Can you put me on to a chemist at Oxford or in London who can deal with it?

The librarian's reply was:

> We have our supplies through Boots in Cornmarket Street. I find however that the stuff is so highly inflammable that it cannot be sent by post. If you are

likely to be in Oxford in the near future I shall be very glad to have a bottle made ready for you from our stock.

'Inflammable' here clearly means extremely flammable! This correspondence suggests that leather dressings were used in the library at some stage, but they are no longer recommended. Current conservation guidance is to avoid all kinds of leather dressing, as the ingredients will dry out your leather over time, and pests like to feed on some of them. If your books are in good condition, they don't need it, and if they are not the binding can be protected with one of the options discussed in the next chapter, such as a polyester wrapper or a box.

Smoke

Naudé was worried about smoke, recommending that your library be heated with a 'stove or chimney, in which nothing must be consumed save wood, which will burn without smoke'. Smoke can degrade bindings, make paper brittle and warp your books. It can stain, and will also leave a smell on the books. Some people love the smell of old books. What they are probably smelling is either the residue of leather dressings, the vanilla scent left by the breaking down of lignin in the wood pulp used for books in the nineteenth and twentieth centuries in place of linen rags, or the lingering smell of wood or tobacco smoke. Some even go to great lengths to recreate the smell of books. In a recent Bodleian exhibition, *Sensational Books*, scent was extracted from a selection of older volumes and analysed so that it could be synthetically recreated and sniffed by exhibition visitors in place of being able to smell the books themselves in their glass cases.

Handling

> let there be a mature decorum in opening and closing of volumes, that they may neither be unclasped with precipitous haste, nor thrown aside after inspection without being duly closed; for it is necessary that a book should be much more carefully preserved than a shoe.
>
> Richard de Bury, *Philobiblon*

The greatest risk to your books is almost certainly how they are handled. Many visitors to libraries assume that gloves are worn when handling special collections. The white cotton gloves that loom large in people's minds are definitely not recommended, as they snag and make fingers clumsy, especially turning pages. At work I wear nitrile gloves made of synthetic rubber to handle embroidered and metal bindings, and engraved copperplates, as these are especially vulnerable to the oils on our hands. But for all other books, clean dry hands are thought to be safest. Be careful, too, of how you take your books from the shelves, how you open and hold them, and how you put them down.

Most of our books now do not have clasps, but we can still be mindful of how we open and close them. Try not to force covers back further than they want to go. If the binding is too tight to hold open comfortably, you could use a book rest: libraries use book cushions, or foam wedges that hold the book open to a maximum of 140 degrees, but can be adjusted downwards depending on how well a book opens. Pages can then be safely weighted down with lead weights known as snakes (see Appendix for supplies of rests and snakes). You can also find wooden book rests with pegs at the front to hold a book – such as a cookbook – open to the page you need. These are fine for robust books whose spines open comfortably to 180 degrees.

Avoid putting your book face down with its pages open: use a bookmark instead. And if you need to have lots of books open at once, try not to stack them open on top of one another. Our forebears had a curious solution to this very problem, known as the book wheel. This large wooden contraption held multiple books open at the same time, and could be rotated as needed.

Keep your elbows off your open books, and try not to fall asleep on them. Finally, don't sit on your books, or use them to prop up heavy things or keep doors open. We used a stack of Yellow Pages as foot rests when we were children learning the piano. That is just about acceptable. Less so Alfred Hackman, a librarian at the Bodleian in the nineteenth century. Hackman was, apparently, a man of short stature. He was compiling a catalogue of all the Bodleian's printed books, and his chair was too low for the desk, so he sat on a large eighteenth-century volume of German history, the *Chronicon Gotwicense*, for some thirty years. The book, bound in vellum, has a distinctly bottom-shaped slope at its centre, where Hackman slid on and off it over decades. He was, by accounts, dismayed when the catalogue was printed and he realized he had forgotten to include the *Chronicon*.

Bookmarks

Turning down the corner of a page to mark your spot will do permanent damage to your book. Use a bookmark: ideally, a slip of acid-free paper. As with the advice above on cuttings, try not to use till receipts or slips made of cheap acidic paper. A library anecdote that no one can quite pin down any more recounts a rasher of bacon being used as a bookmark; this would have left such a horribly greasy residue that it seems hard to imagine it true. On a more elevated note, one of the finest bookmarks in the Bodleian was made for the embroidered Elizabethan Bible mentioned above, of red silk, and embroidered with sequins and silver thread. The Bodleian has ten boxes of bookmarks in the John Johnson Collection of printed ephemera, including a couple of advertisements for cod liver oil in the shape of cod; an advertisement for Pears soap that is a bookmark, paper knife, magnifier and temperature conversion chart all in one; and a Pears bookmark in the shape of glasses, which fit on top of the face-shaped advertisement.

If you don't have acid-free slips, select as slender a bookmark as you can, avoiding thick wooden, metal, leather or plastic ones, or any with a section that slots over the leaf like a large paperclip, as these will disfigure the leaves and damage the binding.

Common Conservation Issues

THIS CHAPTER CONSIDERS DAMAGE your books might already have suffered, and what to do (or not to do) about it. In general, repairs of any books that are or might be valuable (whether in a monetary or sentimental sense) should be undertaken by qualified conservators, or at least by a reliable restorer, and you should leave anything you are unsure about to a professional. Some conservators offer free appraisals, and you can find an accredited one with Icon. As professional repairs can be costly (hourly rates for a conservator start from around £45), it might be better to do nothing rather than have you or someone unqualified mess up a repair.

Some home repair guides will suggest all sorts of things that would make a conservator shudder: how about sanding away inscriptions, or covering them up with liquid paper? The basic principle underlying modern conservation is that any repairs to a book should be reversible, so things such as sanding and liquid paper are to be avoided, along with other rogues we'll meet below. While there are some versions of treatments that conservators undertake that could be attempted at home for modern books of no particular value, it is often better simply to prevent further damage to your books.

Foxing

These brown spots on the pages and on some covers are generally caused by the way low-quality paper is stored. The flaw is already in the paper, but only brought out by conditions such as adverse humidity. If you have a book that is foxed, you can minimize further foxing by keeping it in an environment that is cool and low in humidity. But it can't be reversed, and the marks cannot be removed without invasive and expensive treatment. Institutional libraries do acquire books with foxing, resigning themselves to this imperfection, but confident that their storage systems will stop the foxing from worsening. They don't generally attempt to remove it.

If you are considering buying a book that is foxed (as is very common for books from the nineteenth and twentieth centuries), be aware that it can affect its value. Make sure the aesthetic effect won't spoil your enjoyment of the book. Just because one copy is foxed doesn't mean all in that edition will be too, as storage conditions vary so much. Libraries such as the Bodleian don't say no to a rare book because of foxing, but, if it is to be a favourite book of yours, you might want to find a copy with minimal foxing. How likely are you to find one, and would you be prepared to pay more? If your answers are positive, then wait for a better one to come along.

Red rot

You will have seen leather-bound books with a crumbling spine or covers that leave a reddish-brown smudge on surfaces and your hands. This is known as red rot, and is caused by tanning processes used in the later 1800s and early 1900s that leave the leather acidic. In poor storage conditions (high relative humidity, high temperature and some environmental pollutants) the leather becomes brittle and crumbles into a powder. Again, it is not something that can be easily fixed, and books with this problem are often given a new spine (a treatment called rebacking). This is costly. A more practical – though temporary – solution might be to cover such a book with a polyester sleeve cut as though it were a dust jacket, or a box. These will help at least to keep the residue off hands, surfaces and surrounding books. As with foxing, you will probably have a threshold for what is manageable or acceptable to you. I use foam book rests at work to support the books I'm cataloguing and I shake them out most days to get rid of the debris from red rot. I'm not prepared to put up with it at home, and would not normally buy or acquire for myself a book with this, just for practical reasons. I don't want my other books, shelves, hands or clothes to be covered in smudges.

Broken spine, hinges, detached covers

With this sort of damage, you could repair or simply protect your book. The choice depends on how you want to use the book, how you want it to look, and what your own skills or budget might be.

Most importantly, you must resist the urge to reach for sticky tape. Even in library collections I've seen sticky tape and parcel tape used to cover broken spines, to reattach covers and boards, and to cover over a broken hinge. Sticky tape degrades over time: it loses its stickiness and leaves residues and marks on your books. If used on endpapers, it can also put pressure on them and cause them to tear. If your book has already been repaired with sticky tape, don't try to take it off. Let it fall off in its own time or get a professional conservator to remove it.

Glue is a better option, though whether you should use it on a spine depends on the type of spine and what is loose. It's acceptable to use everyday materials on your everyday books, so if you have a paperback you could use an EVA glue or even a glue stick. Conservators would always use a wheat starch paste, as it can be easily reversed. You can make this at home; while recipes vary a little, here's the version used at the Bodleian:

> Mix 50 ml of wheat starch paste powder with 200 ml of deionised water (or whatever quantity you like in a ratio of 1:4).
> Cook in a saucepan on a small hotplate on a high heat for 10 minutes, then a medium heat for another 20 minutes, stirring constantly so it doesn't stick.
> It is ready when you have a thick and translucent paste with large elongated bubbles appearing as you

stir. You can test it between finger and thumb, and if it feels sticky, it is ready.

Leave this to cool, then sieve to a smooth consistency as required, adding water if needed.

You can also buy adhesive book cloth that could be used for covering over a broken spine.

What about a book with a broken hinge, where the cover is coming away from the textblock inside the book? Conservators would mend this with a Japanese paper hinge and wheat-starch paste; you could make these with whatever sturdy paper you have to hand, and a stick of glue.

When the covers have come off a book, you could have it repaired, or protect it from further damage. A professional bookbinder or conservator will be able to repair the book by rebacking it – that is, adding a new spine to the original boards and, in some cases, reattaching whatever of the original spine covering can be salvaged. If this is done unprofessionally, and the binding is too tight, it will be difficult to open the book to a comfortable angle. Rebacking often involves adding new endpapers; if yours are particularly old or precious, perhaps with an inscription on them, ask to have these bound in during the rebacking. Bear in mind that the cost of rebacking might be significantly more than the value of the book. Prices start from around £130 for rebacking in cloth, and from about £180 for leather.

When a book has been professionally rebacked, it can be safely handled and used as much as you like, and would be a good option for something valuable that you want to read often. But if this is too expensive, there are a couple of protective measures you could take instead. Libraries use unbleached cloth ties – flat strips of cotton akin to shoelaces – to hold loose covers on books that might be rebacked in a perfect world where money were no obstacle. These ties can be used on paperbacks, as well as cloth or leather bindings. They will remind you that the book is fragile, and hold the spine or covers together when the book is not in use. Tie one or two of these gently around your book, securing it with a bow at the fore-edge. These ties are generally white and might not be beautiful to your eye; brown ones are also available and are less obtrusive. See the Appendix for suppliers.

Another option that does not involve repair but helps to keep a book stable is to have a box made for it. You can order a made-to-measure acid-free cardboard box at a modest cost by sending off the dimensions of your book to a specialist supplier. These boxes are normally grey, so, like the white ties, not the most aesthetically pleasing, but they will offer good protection for your book. The Bodleian uses them for all its special collections, and has a team of in-house box-makers called the Packaging and Design Service (referred to hereafter as PADS). As well as protecting damaged covers or spine and keeping the parts of a broken book together, they keep off dust and offer some protection from water while still allowing the book to breathe. Prices start from around £8, and you can choose buttons or ties to keep them closed for another £2.50. If you are willing to spend more, an attractive option would be a cloth- or even leather-covered clamshell box. Again, these are made to measure, and cloth boxes start from around £150, with perhaps another £10 for gold lettering, and leather boxes from around £360. You can get a slipcase from around £90. You will find a wide variety of prices depending on whether you use an institutional supplier such as PADS or a fancy bindery associated with an expensive book dealer. If your book has a paper binding that you would like to protect, you could create a wrapper out of archival quality paper, and simply fold it around the book (as explained below for polyester wrappers). This will give extra protection with or without a box. You might still want to fasten your book with ties even while in the box, if the covers are loose.

The ABA and PBFA websites recommend bookbinders for repairs, including rebacking of cloth or leather bindings, and custom-made cloth or leather boxes.

Heavy books that sag

If you have a largish book where the textblock is sagging and threatening to tear itself loose at the hinges, you can support it with another type of box called a book shoe. This is a four-sided rather than a six-sided box, allowing the spine to be visible on a shelf, but supporting the book at the back, on the sides and underneath with a low stepped insert. These are generally used for books over about 25 cm high. They can be seen on the shelves in Duke Humfrey's library in the Bodleian. PADS offer them from around £10.

Torn or fragile leaves or dust jackets

In the Middle Ages, when many books were written on parchment (that is, animal skin) rather than paper, tears or imperfections in a leaf were repaired with stitches or staples; there are even some examples of paper tears being repaired with sewing. By the nineteenth century, gummed paper (including the edges of a sheet of postage stamps) was available, and was used for mending tears. If your book has a torn page or dust jacket the most important thing is to stay well away from sticky tape. However tempting it may be, the tape will go yellow over time and damage the paper. If the book is special to you, conservators can repair tears with Japanese tissue and wheat-starch paste; this will make the book safe to handle, and will not damage it in the long run. Some handicraft guides explain how to do this yourself, but I would recommend seeking professional help, as it requires practice, care and equipment such as a light box so that the edges of the tear can be exactly matched.

A sleeve made of acid-free polyester can help to protect damaged dust jackets. You can make one yourself with a bone folder (described above) and a sheet of polyester: cut a piece 10–20 cm higher than the book and about three times as wide; place the book in the middle of this with the spine down and open one of the covers; fold the polyester down over that cover, remove the book and use the bone folder to create this fold; put the book back down and wrap the fold around that same cover, then close the book, turn it over, and fold the polyester over the other cover, remove the book, and, after checking that all is aligned, use the bone folder to create the second fold. You can then trim off the extra height at top and bottom. You can also place fragile or torn single sheet material (advertisements, posters, leaflets) in a polyester sleeve so that it can be held safely and read.

For books with folding plates such as illustrations or maps, as well as repairing tears, a bookbinder or restorer can reinforce these with a fabric backing, if it is something you want to unfold and use often.

Loose leaves

I have also seen leaves that have come loose from a book reattached with sticky tape. Again, this is a bad idea. If your book is an 'ordinary' one, you can try to hinge in a loose leaf with small paper hinges and a glue stick or EVA glue. This would not be suitable for older, valuable or precious books, for which a conservator would again use Japanese paper and wheat-starch paste. You could practise these techniques on broken books from charity shops or bins, but if you don't feel confident, and can't afford a conservator, it might be better to use a cloth tie to hold the loose material inside the closed book; the tie will remind you that the book is fragile and has loose parts. Let's also avoid the 'lip glue', a stick you could carry around and lick as needed to make a portable glue, for which I have an eighteenth-century recipe involving various animal glues and 'sugar-candy'.

Missing leaves

If you have or are thinking of acquiring a book with missing leaves, it might be useful to know how some collectors treat this problem. In the past – and I hope no longer – some collectors and booksellers have sacrificed a book, often one that is in bad condition, or is itself imperfect, and broken it up so that the leaves can be added to other copies with missing leaves, to 'perfect' them. I see this often in antiquarian books, and you can spot it by some leaves being of a notably different size, or having marginal notes that do not appear in the rest of the book, or being glued to another leaf rather than actually bound in. Even longer ago, books with leaves missing had these added in manuscript. This is a much nicer way of dealing with the problem, though on a modern budget one might have to settle for printing out photographs of the missing leaves, if you can find a digitized copy online, or even adding photocopies. They could be hinged in to the relevant place, or bound in if you were having the book rebound. One collection in the Bodleian put together in the second half of the twentieth century is full of books that have their missing parts added in this way. They are not pretty, but they are functional.

Marks from water damage or mould

These can be unsightly; while some treatments are available, none are particularly safe for books. It is better to overlook these, or wait to buy a different copy if it will bother you.

Removing inscriptions and notes

There has been a fashion in the past for making books 'clean' and removing signs of ownership and reading. Inscriptions have been scratched out, bleached, washed, and even cut away. Don't do this, as these are all part of a book's history. Even rubbing out pencil prices or other numbers erases information on the past value of a book and, possibly, which booksellers' hands it has passed through. If you must remove pencil marks, make sure you know what they are first, then do it carefully with a good-quality soft eraser.

To conclude: if in doubt, don't repair your book, but give it some protection against further damage. Remember the restoration of a wall painting in Spain by an untrained parishioner, whose meddling resulted in the mess now known as the 'Monkey Christ'?

Ordering and Listing Your Books

How you arrange your books depends on your space, the number of books and how you intend to use them.

Arrangement on shelves

You probably already have a workable system in place. Mine is a bit haphazard, and includes a mix of runs of books in the same series (Loeb classical texts, hardback Everyman classics), loose groupings either by subject (medieval texts, local history) or by type of book (antiquarian, large books, books by friends), and some authors whose works are all placed together. Other than that, our shelves are chaotic. We end up having several copies of particular works, and it takes a while to find things. Our main problem is limited space and no adjustable shelving, so similar-sized books end up being put together whether or not they make sense as a group. This is probably your main consideration too; however nice it would be to have all works by an author together, even if you have adjustable shelves that can accommodate a variety of book sizes, you won't want to have two spacious shelves of big books next to little ones when you could have one shelf of big books and squeeze in two small shelves in the extra space.

BY SIZE

This is certainly the view taken by many libraries, where expensive storage space must be maximized. The Bodleian's first librarian Thomas James advised ordering collections by size, and the antiquarian books that come into the Bodleian today are still shelved in this way, so that no space is wasted by needing to accommodate a large book next to a small one. Each size bracket allows for books that vary in height by up to 2 inches. This is quite generous, and doesn't work so well at home if you are short of space. Modern hardback monsters at 24 cm high don't fit on the shelves that take our 18 cm

Penguin paperbacks, so we can't have a nice alphabetical run of novels by author.

In an ideal world, size wouldn't matter, and I'd shelve novels alphabetically by author. I would probably break up my matching sets of books to shelve everything else (reference works, poetry, etc.) by subject. If you do have some flexibility with your shelving, and can accommodate a wider range of book sizes shelved together, should you group by author, subject, genre or something else?

BY COLOUR

The actress Gwyneth Paltrow and tidying guru Marie Kondo arrange their books by colour. There seem to be endless images of colour-coordinated shelves on social media, too, so the approach clearly has appeal. Many people have a good visual memory for the colour of a book's cover, and readers in libraries refer with surprising frequency to the colour of a book they are looking for. Bernard I. Palmer and A.J. Wells, who wrote *The Fundamentals of Library Classification* in 1951 (it continues to come out in new editions to this day), give serious consideration to arrangement by colour, though they ultimately dismiss it alongside size as an ephemeral feature that tells us nothing about the book. Their other main problem with it is that a limited spectrum of colours is used for book covers, and individual colour groupings will have too many books in them to make finding something easy. In some of these celebrity libraries it seems that coloured covers (perhaps just dust jackets?) are added to particular books so that they can be shelved together in an appropriate grouping. The binding historian Anthony Hobson bound his reference books in different colours to represent different geographical locations, so that you could see at a glance where the books on French binding gave way to those on German. And colour has been used in much older collections to mark books on different subjects, such as the little sets of books used as travelling libraries: the Venetian diplomat Pietro Duodo used three colours of goatskin to distinguish his books, with red for poetry, theology and philosophy; yellow for medicine; and olive for literature. Other travelling library sets used different coloured ribbons to distinguish books in these same three categories.

Having your books specially bound in a particular colour to match the subjects in your library is not a practical solution for most of us. We must stick with the colours as the publishers intended them. You could still arrange your books by colour, then use a catalogue or list arranged by author or subject to cross-reference where they actually are on the shelves. See more on this below.

BY SUBJECT OR GENRE

You can think of subject in very broad terms, not just content (books about trees) but genre (novels, non-fiction, comics), period (eighteenth-century poetry, or antiquarian books) or language. It's not entirely straightforward – how do you decide on your subjects, and what if some books fit into more than one category? Classification is a scientific and philosophical endeavour, and is a completely fascinating subject. It goes all the way back to ancient Greek thought on the classifying of things more generally, and how to create a hierarchy of subjects and subsections; it is as much about the ideology of a good arrangement as it is a practical solution.

The first printed catalogue of 1605 shows that the books in the Bodleian were arranged by subject in one of four categories – law, medicine, theology and arts – then by size, then grouped into individual presses (that is, a case or set of shelves) by the first letter of the author's surname. The catalogue helped readers to locate a particular book. This has shifted now, and the Bodleian's main shelf mark sequence for newly acquired antiquarian books (with prefix 'Vet.', short for *vetera* – that is, 'old books') is organized first by place of printing (A for Great Britain and Ireland; B for The Netherlands and Belgium; C for Denmark, Norway, Sweden, Iceland; D for Germany, Austria, Switzerland; E for France; F for Italy; G for Spain and Portugal; etc.), then by century or half-century (1 = 1501–1600, 2 = 1601–1640, etc.), then by size (a = 20+ inches, b = 15–20 inches, etc.), followed by a running number. For example, the shelf mark 'Vet. F1 g.3' tells you that the book was printed in Italy between 1501 and 1600, and is quite small, below 3 inches. In this arrangement, authors and titles are completely irrelevant, but you can nicely browse the book stacks for books printed in Germany in the eighteenth century in octavo format. This is quite different from the arrangement of books in 1605, and shows how books serve different purposes to different readerships: the focus moved in the Bodleian's ordering of books from textual content (subjects and authors) to the history of printing (place and date).

Books in the general reference collections at the British Library are stored broadly by subject, with shelf marks giving the location.

ALPHABETICAL, BY AUTHOR

What about ordering your whole collection alphabetically by author, as you might order a collection of CDs by artist? This has a lot of appeal, but will also raise questions, as does the seemingly simple arrangement of uniform CDs once you start organizing them (where to put compilations; how do performers fit in?). In an alphabetical sequence of my books, I would need to place C.S. Lewis's *The Allegory of Love*, a scholarly work on medieval literature, alongside his Narnia books, but it would be more relevant in a section devoted to writings from and about the Middle Ages. I also have less of a memory for the names of authors of reference works than I do for their subject, and can imagine needing to scan all my alphabetical shelves to remember the authors of certain books.

Labels

Once you've decided how to order your books, do you want to label your shelves? Probably not; but a book was printed in Paris in 1773 for just this purpose. J.M. Cels' *Coup-d'œil éclaire d'une bibliothèque* was a hefty book of over 400 leaves of shelf labels. These were printed three to a page, and were ready to be cut out, pasted to wooden dummies and placed on the shelves as a guide to finding different subjects. They covered the five broad areas of theology, law, arts and sciences, literature and history, with countless subdivisions within these, as well as some spare blank labels for you to add anything that wasn't otherwise covered.

Some libraries preferred to note divisions within sections on the spines of the books. The Bodleian used paper labels with letters on them, and there's a wonderful survival of a printed sheet you could buy to do just this. The London printer Bernard Lintot sold a printed broadsheet in the early eighteenth century with labels bearing letters for labelling each shelf, then smaller letters and numbers to paste on the spine of each book. He called it *An alphabetical list of numbers for the better regulating Gentlemens Libraries. Contrivd in such a manner that any Servant who knows his Letters may keep the Books in Order.*

Catalogues and shelf lists

> The mechanical perfection of a library requires an alphabetical catalogue of the whole.
>
> William Gladstone,
> *On Books and the Housing of Them*, 1890

Catalogues tell you what books are in a library, by author, subject or some other organizing principle. A shelf list tells you the exact order of the books as they are on the shelves, grouping them only in so far as they were grouped when placed on those shelves. The first Bodleian catalogue of 1605 was a catalogue and a shelf list all in one. Books were arranged on the shelves by subject and author, and each page of the catalogue corresponded to one press (bookcase). At least one copy was printed on one side of each leaf only, so that it could be pinned up on the end of each press as a guide both to what was there and how to find it. The titles of many old catalogues were often tied to a specific location, so that the books could be found. The *Catalogue of Books in the Closet in the Passage Room next the Pantry in Skipton Castle*, from 1739, is one of my favourites. Most of us will find a catalogue most useful for recording what we have.

The first library catalogue that we know of was made a little over 2,000 years ago by the librarian and poet Callimachus, of the library at Alexandria. Estimates suggest the library held some 500,000 rolls, perhaps equivalent to 100,000 books today. Callimachus' catalogue of it, the *Pinakes*, took up some 120 rolls. Only fragments of it now survive, but it seems to have been arranged by subject and genre, and then by author. Five hundred years ago, some attempts were made to list all known books. Hernando Colón (son of Christopher Columbus) went as far as providing a summary of each book that he listed. In 1545 Conrad Gessner attempted to produce a list of everything that had ever been written, whether published or 'lurking in a library', by learned and unlearned people, ancient or modern or no longer existing. Estimates vary, but he listed somewhere between 10,000 and 15,000 thousand titles. Towards the end of the same century the bookseller and bibliographer Andrew Maunsell attempted a sort of national bibliography with his printed catalogue of English printed books. He says it only contains things he saw, and he leaves room for readers to add to it as they find new books. Maunsell arranged his catalogue in three broad subject areas, and within those, alphabetically, by author's surname (unlike Gessner, who arranged his catalogue by first name).

What sort of catalogue might you use for your books at home? The old-fashioned answer (and still one of the most practical) is a card catalogue. This has been a staple of institutional and private libraries throughout the twentieth century. Buy yourself an index box and some cards, and you have a flexible record of your books that can accommodate new ones easily. If you want to note the location of the book in your house, there's plenty of room to do so. The only downside is that such a list is no use when you are out and about buying books. How often have you bought something you already own? I certainly have, several times. If you want a portable list, consider an electronic one. This could be a simple spreadsheet (Microsoft Excel or Google Sheets); I use these for any book-related projects that require a list of a significant number of books. Spreadsheets are marvellous not just because they are easy to add to, but because they let you reorder your data in any way you want at the click of a mouse. If you want to sort the list one day by date, another by author, or another by place of printing or publisher, you can do so without effort, as long as you've put the information into it. These are columns you might like to consider: title, author, date, printer/publisher, place of printing, illustrator, height, edition, type of binding (hardback/paperback, cloth/leather, colour), along with a column for general notes for special features, such as signed copy, limited edition, and so on.

However, squinting at a spreadsheet on a mobile phone is not my idea of fun, and you might prefer to list your books on an app such as Library Thing. It is more easily used on a mobile device such as a phone, and is particularly good for modern books. If they are modern enough to have a barcode the app will scan and record the information automatically, saving you time listing them. The app is free, and you can view it on your laptop or PC, and have it with you on a smartphone. You can add additional notes to each record, such as when you read it and what you thought of it. An image of the book's cover automatically appears alongside the record, reminding you of its physical aspect.

If you prefer something more romantic than an app or a spreadsheet and don't have a large collection, you could record your books in a notebook. Address books work particularly well, as they are already separated into alphabetical sections, and you could find one to match the scale of your library, or the purpose for which you make it, such as a small portable one to carry around with you, or a large one that stays at home. This could be ruled into columns, but will need to be more limited in what it records: perhaps just author, title, date, publisher. There is an example of such a catalogue in the Bodleian, measuring 6 × 5 cm, that records the Morton collection of miniature books. It is one volume in a set of three, in their own little box; the other two record 'kind donors' in the 1920s and 1930s, and prices for some of the books that were purchased.

If you choose this type of catalogue and are adding to your books, you will have to be content with being in the company of the Bodleian 1605 catalogue and arrange authors under the first letter of their surname, rather than in a strictly alphabetical order, and also to adding other works by that author later in your book as acquired.

If you want an elaborate library catalogue, you could take inspiration from collectors of the past, and have one written out for you, perhaps on parchment, in a fine calligraphic script. Some collectors in the seventeenth century had their library catalogue written up on a parchment roll. Frances Egerton, Countess of

Bridgewater, had one made for her 241 books, on a roll 220 cm long, arranged by subject then author. The jurist Edward Coke had a much larger library, and a much longer roll on which to record it: the catalogue he had drawn up in 1634 stretches for 42 feet.

Leaving Your Mark

Book ownership is transient. Most books have many owners over their lifetime, and we are merely their temporary guardians. Should you, then, mark your ownership or guardianship of a book? As a librarian, I would say yes. A bookseller might advise otherwise, as 'clean' copies are often more appealing to a buyer and command higher prices. There was a fashion in the eighteenth and early nineteenth centuries to cleanse books of all signs of their previous owners. Notes in the margins and ownership marks on title pages and endpapers were washed or bleached, worn away with an abrasive, or even cut out, leaving books damaged and poorer in their transmission of history. These marks of ownership are now increasingly valued by collectors and libraries. This chapter suggests some of the many ways in which you might mark your books in a sensitive way.

One of the main marks institutional libraries want to make in their books is of course the shelf mark (also known as the class mark). You probably don't need shelf marks for your books, unless you have a very large collection. If you do, these can either be written in pencil in the book, or on an acid-free slip of paper tucked inside it. You might also consider an inventory number, which allows you to cross-reference to your catalogue or book list.

As a general rule, record your name, ownership mark or shelf mark on a book's endpapers, rather than the title page. A decent soft pencil (B or 2B) is always a safe option: as long as you don't press too hard, it can be removed later on if a future owner prefers. Graphite pencil seems to last fairly well; it has been used since the late eighteenth century, and plenty of examples survive from the early nineteenth century. As well as shelf marks, libraries use pencil to write accession numbers and sometimes catalogue reference numbers in their older or special books, and booksellers use it to record their price codes, stock numbers and notes to themselves.

Inks

There is no problem in using ink of a decent quality (no biro or felt tip) to write your name into your ordinary books. But what about your special books? Should you write in ink in those? Some might consider it an act of vandalism to mark a rare and valuable old book with a modern inscription, especially if you are a person of no particular note. As a librarian, though, I want to see all of a book's owners, especially if the book is old and rare and valuable. While some caution is required, particularly if you are collecting for financial return, and have acquired something very valuable, inscribing your name elegantly on a book's endpapers in a good ink is acceptable. Don't be tempted to inscribe the title page.

Choose your ink carefully. I have a lovely turquoise ink that is a joy to write with, but it fades quickly even when not exposed to light: notes I made just four or five years ago as I attempted to learn Old English grammar have completely vanished from the page, as they have from my memory. If you want a bold colour for your inscriptions, choose a good-quality brand of artists' ink or an ink made by a specialist fountain-pen company. I have used coloured inks for copying out poems into small notebooks, and these have not yet faded the way the turquoise ink has, so I think it depends very much on the brand. I use Winsor & Newton for my coloured inks, and you can find wonderful metallic ones in their range, but Quink, Cross or Mont Blanc for my regular blue or black. None of these appear to have problems with fading.

Iron gall ink was one of two main types of ink used for centuries, but because it's acidic it can – and has – burned into books inscribed with it. Somewhat nicer are the glittery metallic residues sometimes left behind by early inks, such as that used to record inventory numbers in the books that belonged to Henry VIII. Early books on penmanship and books of household management often include recipes for ink, including gold ones. And of course there are scented inks. I have a violet-scented one, but the scent fades quickly once the ink is on paper. Charles Lutwidge Dodgson (aka Lewis Carroll) liked purple ink for inscribing his books, though I don't imagine his was scented.

Inscriptions

The most obvious way to record your guardianship of a book is to write your name in it. But should you add anything else – and if so, what?

Suppose your book still survives in three hundred years. Its readers (scholars, librarians or later owners) will want your inscription to reveal all kinds of details about how you came to own it. Was it a gift, or a purchase? If a purchase, where and when was it, and how much did you pay? These are all questions that are becoming increasingly of interest, as these pieces of isolated information can be gathered together to provide a mass of data about book ownership in the past. Including the name of the bookshop or seller will cause great delight to future historians of the book trade, and so, too, will a note of your profession. Goldsmiths seemed particularly keen on mentioning their job when inscribing their books. Peter Blake, an English goldsmith in the sixteenth century, inscribed his copy of an English translation of Erasmus with a note that he was a goldsmith. He might be the man of this name examined in the trial of Mary Queen of Scots about a jewel Babington pawned with him. Arnold Weelen, who was a director of the mint at Liège, did the same in the eighteenth century with his copy of a money-changer's guide to currency printed a century earlier. Being a goldsmith who owned books was clearly something to be proud of. Older inscriptions often include the owner's age, academic qualifications, affiliation (university, church, monastery or Inn of Court). It's up to you how far to go with this! The following was written by two boys in a volume of Cicero published in Venice:

> Bassano Feraro, called Latino, from the place of Gombeto in the diocese of Cremona owns this book, which cost 2 and 10 and I think he bought it from the bookseller in Cremona under the Palace in 1592 on the 2nd day of February: I Antonio Galli his dearest friend confirm the above.

You might even want to develop your own book signature, monogram or motto. Certain phrases were commonly used alongside inscriptions, such as: 'Anne is the true owner of this book; God give her grace on it to look.' Early-modern book owners liked to add a motto to their inscription. Usually of the lofty and inspiring kind, there are some more casual ones that I find amusing. How about *Medio tutissimus* ('Safest in the middle') or *Nec elata nec deiecta* ('Neither raised up nor cast down'), or the general and slightly creepy *Amo* ('I love')? Some are amusingly arrogant, such as Anne of Denmark's *La mia grandezza viene dal eccelso* ('My greatness comes from on high'), or blunt, *Vincere vel mori* ('Win or die'). Others are hopeful – *Bons temps viendra* ('Good times will come') – or just odd: *Nuda senectus* ('forlorn old age').

Gift inscriptions

I am so grateful to the various people who have written in books they've given me. My earliest inscription is in A.A. Milne's *When We Were Very Young* ('To Francesca Galligan on her first birthday...'); some are from grandparents no longer with us (*Folk & Fairy Tales*, 'To Francesca. Best wishes on your 7th birthday, Nanna'); many are from parents and partner, recording birthdays and anniversaries (Lewis Carroll, *Illustrated Works* ('To our darling Francesca for your 8th birthday'). Each of these makes a book immeasurably more precious to me, reminding me of when I received it, and of beloved friends and relatives. I wish all my books told these stories. If you are giving someone a book, whether a cheap paperback, a special edition gift book, or something valuable, do write a note of your gift in it for the person to enjoy in future years.

Book curses

A book curse is another excellent way to mark your ownership and encourage a borrower to return your book. It could be anything from a simple warning, such as this one written into *Pictures of English History*, in 1809 – 'Absolom Dell. His Book. Don't steal.' – to ones that promise a little more vengeance, such as 'he that steals this book away shall in a hempen halter sway', from 1773, and this on a similar theme, translated loosely from French as 'if I lose this book and it's returned, I'll give you good wine; if not you'll hang by the neck'.

Ink stamps

Some owners mark their books with a personalized ink stamp. These were especially popular from the later eighteenth century in Britain, though examples date back to at least the sixteenth century. While these sorts of mark are more likely to be familiar to you from institutional libraries, many private libraries have also used them. There are websites and stationers that even allow you to design your own personal one.

All books entering Bodleian collections, including antiquarian books, are stamped in ink for security reasons, and much energy has gone into finding a suitable ink to use for this. It probably doesn't matter whether you use a pre-inked stamp or an ink pad on your regular books, as long as you use a good-quality one. If you want to stamp an older or more precious book, it would be best to do this on an endpaper.

Blind-embossed stamps

For some, an ink stamp is too obvious a mark in a book, and an embossed stamp that raises the paper in a pattern with lettering that can be read under raking light is preferable. The Bodleian has a stamp of this kind that is used on some modern artists' books. However, these stamps require practice. It is quite easy to rip pages with them, or stamp too vigorously and create holes, so use with caution, on an endpaper.

Bookplates and book labels

Labels stuck into books to record an owner's name date back to the fifteenth century. These are usually made of paper, and occasionally of parchment or thin leather tooled in gold. All sorts of techniques – woodcuts, engravings, lithographs, photography – have been used to create these over the centuries. An early example is a large woodcut bookplate by Lucas Cranach the Elder, from the first decade of the 1500s, with a large female figure holding the coat of arms of a German jurist, diplomat and humanist named Christoph Scheurl. It is unusual for its size (the leaf measures at least 30 × 20 cm, while the printed area is 16.5 × 12.7 cm) and hand-coloured.

The design of these took off into all sorts of new directions in the eighteenth and nineteenth centuries. The sculptor Anne Damer used a bookplate designed by Agnes Berry to mark her ownership in the eighteenth century. Walter Crane designed bookplates for owners including May Morris; and artists Kate Greenaway, Alice B. Woodward and Marion Reed all designed them in the late nineteenth and first half of the twentieth centuries. The artist, photographer and folklorist William J. Thoms used a photographic bookplate in the 1860s/70s of himself seated at a table, reading books. There are many societies dedicated to bookplates and their history and there is even a collectors' market, so you will see them loose at book fairs.

If you'd like your own bookplates to mark your books, you can buy any manner of them, either gummed to be moistened and stuck in or already sticky-backed. You can even have your own printed, and the Society of Wood Engravers might provide some inspiration for this. Most bookplates will not be of archival quality, and could discolour over time, or fall out having lost their stickiness, so look for good-quality ones. The Bodleian uses bookplates to mark donations, but these are stuck with wheat paste into the box that is made for each book that becomes part of Special Collections, rather than directly into the book itself. At home I use gummed and sticky ones for my books. I have used these in seventeenth-century books, but only where the endpapers are modern replacements. As with inscriptions, it is best to place bookplates inside the upper cover or on an endpaper, rather than on the back of the title page. Some collectors stick their bookplate over that of the previous owner. This seems a shame, as that owner then becomes obscure. I prefer to see several bookplates in a single book, even when the endpapers become covered in them.

Making notes

> impudent boys are to be specially restrained from meddling with books, ... wherever they perceive the broadest margin about the text, they furnish it with a monstrous alphabet, or their unchastened pen immediately presume to draw any other frivolous thing whatever, that occurs to their imagination. There the Latinist, there the sophist, there every sort of

> unlearned scribe tries the goodness of his pen, which
> we have frequently seen to have been most injurius to
> the fairest volumes, both as to utility and price.
>
> Richard de Bury, *Philobiblon*

Books in historic collections contain many sorts of everyday markings, as writing surfaces such as paper or parchment were scarce and expensive. Margins were used to test pens, to practise alphabets and to draft letters or notes. Richard de Bury disapproves of these, particularly pen trials and alphabets, noting that these can make the books less appealing and less valuable. This is the advice many booksellers and collectors might also give. But marginal notes are important, and can and should have a place in book collections. Refrain from making your own marginal notes in any books of historical value, or particular age or monetary value, or use pencil neatly if you must mark them. But in your modern working books, why not make significant marginal notes permanent with a good ink? We would have lost so much of interest if early book owners had not written in their books.

Early-modern readers were taught how to annotate books in ways that helped to navigate a text with headings, numbering and key words to the margins. In

1612 John Brinsley wrote that annotations could be made with ink, pencil or fingernail. It seems that women in particular used drypoint or fingernail, making their marks in books much less obvious than those of male readers. Anne Boleyn is thought to have marked her margins with her fingernail, and a much earlier case has recently been explored in the Bodleian, where markings scratched in an eighth-century manuscript of the Acts of the Apostles were made by a woman named Eadburg. Various photographic techniques have revealed that she not only wrote her name in the margins, probably with a metal stylus, but also made sketches of faces, perhaps using the outline of her finger as a template.

Some of my favourite reading moments have been comments written into books by long-gone owners. Top of this list, without a doubt, is Henry VIII adjusting the Tenth Commandment on coveting one's neighbour's wife: it is only a sin, he adds, when done 'wrongly or unjustly'. Another favourite is a copy of J.R.R. Tolkien's edition of *Sir Gawain and the Green Knight* that was owned by C.S. Lewis. Lewis has added copious notes to the margins, as well as drawings of a suit of armour, spear and fortifications. Notes and drawings don't have to be by notable people to be interesting. A reader of a 1631 book of curious facts underlines every instance of the word 'gout' in the index, as well as writing in remedies for burns and rheumatism. In a seventeenth-century scientific work in English a reader writes in Latin next to a passage about animals and dreams that 'even a dog barks at footprints of hares in its sleep'. Reading these slightly odd observations opens a direct link to past readers and what mattered to them. Some readers liked to note their progress through a book. A wonderful example has just come to light in the Bodleian, owned by Lady Anne Clifford. Marginal notes in her own and her secretary's hand record when in 1670, by whom, and at which of her four castles passages from *A Mirour for Magistrates*, an important source for Shakespeare, were read out to her.

Books large and small have been used to record things that were of personal importance: historical and family events such as births and deaths, lists and inventories, debts and expenses, diaries, sketches and poetry. We're all familiar with the idea of the family Bible as the one reliable book that seemed a solid and safe place to record family history as it happened. Portable calendars in book form also offered a convenient place to record diaries and personal events.

Frances Wolfreston used hers in the 1670s to record a long succession of births and deaths, as well as more mundane household affairs such as 'sold the gray mare' and 'I bot my dish ketell the 14 of this month'.

Books were also a good place to keep records of expenses, money owned or inventories of goods. A reader of Aulus Gellius's *Attic Nights* in the seventeenth century has made a list of linens at the end of the book: 'A surplice, a shirt, three bands, one cap, one napkin, one towel, one Handchercheife, three payre of cuffes'. Perhaps it's a packing list for a trip away? Noblewoman Frances Egerton used her books to record notes of making pillowcases, and Sir Christopher Hatton used his to note the number of deer culled at the royal park at Eltham over the winter of 1578, where he was keeper.

These sorts of notes are fascinating in their own right, and sometimes record opinions as well as facts. The owner of a catalogue for an auction of books in 1850 notes that one lot was purchased by a man's 'awful son'. An early reader of Jane Austen's *Sense and Sensibility* wrote scathingly in the margin 'More absolute Trash was never written than in the present work.' And there are so many examples of censorship, whether the diligent crossing out of words including 'pope', 'Mary' or 'Thomas Becket' on religious grounds, or of material more generally deemed unsuitable. An encyclopaedia for children published in 1789–90 has two pages on childbirth stuck together with blobs of wax so that they cannot be read, and instructions written on them that they should not be unsealed. Other references to childbirth in the text have also been crossed out.

Margins and endpapers offered space for useful information that could be returned to. In the early seventeenth century, one John Smith didn't feel confident in his use of Greek numbers, so he wrote himself a chart on the title page of his 100-year-old copy of Dioscorides' medical works, then used the chart to write his name and the date in Greek. The blank space in books could also capture creative moments, from copying other people's poems out (such as the reader who wrote out lines from Shakespeare's *Lucrece* into his copy of a text on economics while Shakespeare himself was still alive) to composing your own, such as the verses on mortality written into an edition of Vergil's works from the early sixteenth century, which begin 'Like as [the] Damaske Rose you see'.

Lending your books

It is nice to lend friends books, but only if they look after them and give them back. I'm guilty of accidentally keeping one or two that have been lent to me, but I think I've lost more than I've gained. One way of encouraging your books to come back to you is to mark your ownership in them very clearly, as a constant reminder to the guilty person of where they belong.

In fact you should *only* consider lending your books when you've marked your ownership of them in some way. You might want to keep a list of loans, too. Frances Wolfreston used her almanacs to keep track of books she lent to friends. You might heed the advice of Gabriel Naudé:

> [lending] should not be for above a fortnight or three weeks at most, and ... the *Library-keeper* be careful to register in a Book destin'd for this purpose, and divided by Letters Alphabetically, whatsoever is so lent out to one or other, together with the date of the day, the form of the Volume, and the place and year of its impression; and all this to be subscribed by the Borrower, this to be cancel'd when the Book is returned, and the day of its reddition put in the margent, thereby to see how long it has been kept; and that such as shall have merited by their diligence and

care in conserving of Books, may have others the more readily lent to them.

> Naudé, *Advis pour dresser une bibliothèque*

You could keep a notebook for this, or mark loans in pencil in your library catalogue. Card catalogues are good for this too, as you can extract a card for any book lent, and keep it at the front of the box holding the cards.

Special Finishes for Special Books

Full goodly bound in pleasaunt coverture,
Of Damas, Sattin, or els of velvet pure
                Sebastian Brant, *Ship of Fools*, 1509

I F YOU LIKE the idea of a special personalized copy of a favourite text, this chapter is for you. You might not have thought about customizing books, assuming they come as they come, with covers, ornament or illustration determined by the publisher. But things have not always been this way. Over the centuries books have been offered with different finishes for customers with variously sized pockets, and many of these options are still available today.

Bindings

Covers only became an integral part of a publication relatively recently, in the late eighteenth and early nineteenth centuries. Before that, the sheets of paper on which a book was printed were unbound, and offered by stationers or booksellers with a range of covers and finishes from the basic and cheap to expensive and highly decorated options. An extraordinary survival – a printed advertisement from a London bookseller in 1619 – lists some of the options that were available, with prices. This sheet would have been displayed in the shop, so that customers could choose from a range of bindings. A basic binding of sheepskin without decoration (suitable, the advertisement says, for various practical books such as grammars, small editions of the New Testament, or classical texts) cost 2–4 pence, and was a relatively cheap option. You could go upmarket and choose a better-quality leather (calf or goatskin) and have it decorated with gold tooling, 'Bookes of all sorts gilt, edges and corners', which cost 8 pence for a small book of psalms and up to 15 shillings for a large church Bible. Sometimes these binding options were even printed in the book itself:

> This booke is to be solde by the imprinter in queres [that is, unbound] for two shilynges & sixe pence, and not above, bound in parchement or forell, for three shillynges and .iiii. pence and not above: and bounde in lether, in paper boordes or claspes, for foure shillynges and not above.
>
> *Boke of Common Praier*, Richard Grafton, London, 1552

If your book was already bound, you could still change it to suit your own tastes, and this was a popular thing to do particularly in the seventeenth and eighteenth centuries: some collectors liked to embellish an existing binding, adding their coat of arms or more elaborate tooling, or labels or spine titles; others preferred to remove it entirely and have their books rebound so that they all looked similar, either in a preferred colour or with their coat of arms or favourite tooling. Samuel Pepys mentions just this in his diary:

> My bill for the rebinding of some old books to make them suite with my study, cost me, besides other new books in the same bille, 3£; but it will be very handsome
>
> Samuel Pepys, *Diary*, Friday 3 February 1664/5

Rebinding is not something most conservators or librarians would recommend for an older book, as it changes its history in a dramatic way, often taking with it all signs of past owners, readers and clues to where it has been. For older books, small repairs and the protective measures mentioned in Chapter 5 – such as commissioning a tailor-made box – would be best. But if you have a favourite modern book in an ordinary binding (not a first or important early edition), or a household book such as a favourite cook book, your library catalogue or a visitors' book, you might want to commission a special binding for it. You could even design your own binding tool for use on your books or their boxes. Today, for a binding in quarter-leather (with just the spine made of leather, and the boards covered in cloth or paper), you might pay from about £180; for half-leather (spine and corners of boards in leather), from about £210; for full leather, from about £280 upwards, depending on the type of leather and whether you want tooling and a title on the spine. Goatskin has traditionally been used for the finest bindings, and will be more expensive than calfskin, which is in turn more expensive than sheepskin. At a smart place such as the Chelsea Bindery, you will pay from £650 upwards for a goatskin binding. You could commission a binding from a designer bookbinder that reflects or illustrates aspects of the text, or depicts something deeply personal. An organization such as the Designer Bookbinders society can help you to get started. You can browse their members' work online, and visit fairs to see examples of what can be done and find a style that suits you. Bindings of this sort could be as elaborate as you want, with leathers of different colours making patterns or illustrations or just about anything you can imagine, and will cost from about £500 to several thousand pounds. A particularly elaborate example was made by the high-end London binders Sangorski & Sutcliffe in the early twentieth century for an edition of the *Rubáiyát* of Omar Khayyám. The binding was adorned with peacocks, made of jewels and gold, and referred to as the 'Great Omar'. It was sold at auction and sent over to its new owner in New York. The ship carrying it was the *Titanic,* and the book sank with the ship. Sangorski & Sutcliffe – along with another fine binding firm, Zaehnsdorf – is now part of Shepherds Bookbinders, which bound the Bible used for King Charles's coronation in Westminster Abbey in 2023. It takes commissions for bindings as well as for conservation and restoration work. If your budget is limited, you might like to take a course in bookbinding, and have a go yourself.

DECORATED EDGES

Bindings include features other than just the covers of a book. Edge decoration has also been popular for centuries, and there are many finishes to choose from that can also be applied today. At a modest level, the edges of the textblock (that is, the part of a book that you can flick) would be coloured with a plain block of colour such as red, blue or yellow; or a marbled pattern or coloured swirls of paste could be applied. A more expensive finish saw gold leaf applied to create gilt edges, and a pattern could be impressed into those edges, known as gauffering. There are some wonderfully elaborate examples of gilt and gauffered edges from the sixteenth and early seventeenth centuries, often on French books for royal owners, and sometimes parts of these were even painted. Paint was also used directly on the textblock edges, and ranges from the almost home-made example of Elizabeth Brodridge, whose name is painted on the edges of a Bible from 1660 along with roses and tulips, to books in the Pillone Library that bear portraits of their authors. A version of this sort of decoration is currently popular in publishing, with new hardback fiction sometimes issued in a special edition with 'sprayed' edges. Edge decorations could also be hidden, and the family of booksellers Edwards of Halifax (one of whom was advertised as an 'exotic bookseller' and seemed to be a 'gentleman spy') excelled in this technique in the eighteenth and early nineteenth centuries. When the book is closed the fore-edges look plain; when you fan them out, a painted scene, usually a landscape, becomes visible. I had a go at creating a very basic one of these on the edges of a National Trust handbook. The pages need to be fanned out and held in place with a clamp while you draw or paint on them. Mine wasn't terribly successful, and I could see traces of the ink when the book was closed. A layer of gilding was usually added after a fore-edge had been painted to get round this problem.

You can see some contemporary examples of this by the artist Martin Frost on his website. He also takes commissions.

ENDPAPERS

The endpapers of a book (that is, the inside of the cover and the paper between the covers and the text) can also be customized in a binding made to your commission. While occasionally made of parchment, silk or tooled leather, they are most often made of paper. Papers decorated with different techniques have been made as endpapers and covers for book bindings for centuries, with patterns swirled in paste, stencilled in bright colours, marbled or block-printed. If you would like to see the range of these, there is a Facebook group dedicated to them, with over 8,000 members, called We Love Endpapers. They can be playful, beautiful, pictorial or just decorative. Maps are popular, for example on the endpapers of *Winnie the Pooh*, or Middle Earth inside the covers of *The Hobbit*. Occasionally endpapers also disguise things, such as a speech from the scaffold by a Jacobite named James Shepperd, hidden in the wooden boards of a Greek New Testament, now in the Bodleian.

CLASPS AND TIES

> His studie has commonly handsome shelves, his books neate silke strings, which he shewes to his father's man, and is loth to vntye or take downe for fear of misplacing.
>
> John Earle, *Microcosmographie*, 1628

Other elements of a binding you might want to consider are clasps and ties. Fastenings of various sorts have been used to hold books closed over the centuries, helping to protect the textblock and prevent the leaves and boards from warping. These have been made with a variety of materials such as silk, linen, leather, bone, silver, gold, brass, and sometimes enamelled, or bejewelled, and have become largely decorative in more recent centuries. Cloth ties were usually just of one colour, but occasionally we find striped ones, or two colours used diagonally, so each tie had two different coloured ribbons. Some collectors even matched the ties on their books to the colours on their coat of arms. One elaborate example in the Bodleian purports to be made of the garter ribbon of Charles I; while there is no firm evidence for this, it is certainly an extravagant example of unusually wide ties made of blue silk. Institutional libraries didn't like leather and cloth ties very much, as readers forgot to do them up, leaving the shelves looking messy. The Bodleian had rules requiring its readers to fasten the ties when they had finished with a book, and even resorted to paying extra staff (some 'poore Schollars') to tie them up in advance of important visits. Eventually they were all chopped off to solve the problem.

Metal clasps were suited to books bound in wooden boards, and started to decline in the sixteenth century as pasteboard replaced wood. There was a revival of these in the late nineteenth century, as the Victorians liked to recreate much older bindings, adding clasps and ties such as the coloured cloth ones on William Morris's parchment bindings for his Kelmscott Press. There is a brand of notebook today that reproduces versions of fine bindings from past centuries, often adding metal clasps to these, and ties are still used on some children's books. I have a lovely pop-up volume of Christmas carols that we carefully tie and untie each Christmas. You could no doubt have some added to a special binding if you wanted them, though metal clasps can cause trouble in collections, as they can catch on surrounding books and rip their covers. If you have books with clasps, be careful not to pack them tightly on the shelves, and perhaps consider a box or book shoe to protect surrounding volumes.

METAL BINDINGS AND BOOK FURNITURE

Round bosses in the corners and centre of a book's covers initially served a practical function, to protect large books from being scratched and torn. This practical function gave way to a decorative one, and flat metal centrepieces and corner pieces were added to embellish books. Margaret Tudor had a green velvet binding with gilt silver bosses in the shape of Tudor roses, each bearing a letter that spelled out her name. Elizabeth I had centrepieces of gold with her arms and a crowned Tudor rose on an edition of the New Testament, fixed on with gold nails. These were also revived to some extent in the nineteenth century, and you can currently buy metal pieces online to protect the corners of books. I didn't know there was any vogue for these. Although a quick browse suggests there are endless decorative possibilities, they appear to be mostly sold in large packs, and probably not of great quality. I doubt you would want to have these in your hand or risk them damaging your books. Searches for centrepieces and bosses, by contrast, don't yield any results, presumably because they would be harder to attach to a modern binding than a cornerpiece.

Illumination and decoration of text

As well as choosing the type of binding, a customer could also have finishing touches added to the text by hand. In manuscripts and early printed books, places were often left for coloured or illuminated initials, borders, coats of arms and illustrations, or, more modestly, headings or paragraph marks could be added to the text in red or blue. These embellishments depended on a customer's preference and what she or he could afford.

While these became less common as printing managed to reproduce many of these effects – initials and borders could be cut in wood, printed alongside the text and reused in other editions or works – a customer could still have a printed book hand-illuminated, or, on a more basic level, the title underlined by hand in red ink, and a red margin drawn around every page of text. This framing of the text in red was especially popular in France in the sixteenth century for finely bound books, and lingered in England over the seventeenth. Royal books were often finished in this way, such as the 'travelling libraries' of the Stuart princes Henry and Charles. The red frame around every page underlines the special and lavish nature of these gifts.

William Morris wanted to recreate the feeling of a medieval illuminated manuscript with the books he published from his Kelmscott Press, and used printed wood-engraved borders and illustrations to embellish his books, where once these decorative features would have been added by hand.

If you would like to have a book decorated or illuminated, the Calligraphy and Lettering Arts Society has a list of its fellows, and the Society of Scribes & Illuminators lists members who take commissions. Illuminators, along with fine binders, will prefer to work with an unbound book. You can buy books in sheets (that is, unbound) from many private presses.

Getting Rid of Books

During a COVID-19 lockdown I watched as the contents of a house were emptied into a skip, including plants and brass stands, vintage tools, cabinets, bowls and umbrella stands. But the books – several shelves of paperbacks – were loaded into a car and driven away. I was relieved to see that something was saved, though I suspect the things in the skip were much more valuable. It is overwhelming to be confronted with clearing a house, especially that of a close relative or friend, and hard to find time to get rid of things usefully. Bundling books into a skip might seem in many cases to be the easiest – perhaps even the only – option. But there are alternatives, and this chapter will help you to find some of them, whether you are weeding your own books to make a bit more space for new ones, or getting rid of someone else's collection.

Books as memory

You might use your books as a way of remembering what you've read. I certainly do, and the physical aspect of books seems to evoke a strong visual memory. Until very recently I've been keeping novels that I know I won't read again, just because otherwise I will forget their existence. Looking at a book's cover is often enough for me to remember the basics of a novel in a way that the title on its own does not. But most modern homes don't allow for this kind of indulgence. So if, like me, this is one of your reasons for keeping books on shelves that are now full, you could explore other ways of remembering what you've read. I kept a list of my reading as a child, and started this up again a couple of years ago. I only record author, title and a general comment (usually my verdict on the novel, in one word). This is not quite enough to prompt a memory of the plot for me, so when I start my next notebook I will include a couple of sentences that summarize it. You could even keep photographs of the covers of your books in an album on a smartphone, to prompt your visual memory after the books have gone to a new home.

Making space for new books

I can't tell you how to make space on your shelves for new books, as only you can work out what to part with. For me, novels I haven't particularly enjoyed are now low-hanging fruit, and I'm happy to see them go, even if that risks forgetting their existence. Reference works and 'classics' can be harder cases. When we moved into our house the previous owner left us some of her books. This was wonderful, as our tastes overlapped, and we had plenty of shelf space. We kept everything. But for the past couple of years we've had three piles of books – towers, really – on our stairs, growing ever higher and causing a minor safety hazard. In an attempt to get all these off the floor, we've been reappraising the books on the shelves. We have two copies of *Three Men in a Boat*, *Northanger Abbey*, *Vanity Fair*, *Middlemarch* and Camus's *Plague* (who would have foreseen how handy it would be during our own plague to have a spare one to lend to family and friends?). Any cheap modern paperbacks would be the thing to get rid of here, but our copies are mostly in hardback: nice little Everyman editions from the 1920s, 1930s and 1940s, less nice bigger Everyman classics from the 1990s, and nice little Oxford editions. For now, I think we are keeping them. I find the reference books more difficult. We are keeping dictionaries of English literature, music and philosophy as they are good standard reference works, and the children might use them for their studies. I've not opened them since they passed to us, but I keep imagining a future in which they might be useful. I do use my *Oxford Classical Dictionary* even though I have access to an updated electronic version. Having grown up before the internet and electronic books, I find reference volumes reassuring, and I like to imagine a future in which I am retired, with plenty of time to read things that might require access to reference works. Surely a day will come when I'll be glad to have my volume on Italian verse forms to hand?

Breaking up of libraries

You might be downsizing, moving house, retiring and having to empty an office of books, or dealing with a collection from a friend or relative. Weeding your shelves to make space for new books is one thing. Getting rid of a whole collection, whether your own or someone else's, is quite another.

When I see a private collection come up for sale, I always feel a pang of sadness for the person who put it together. It is something that has been carefully assembled with specialist subject knowledge over many years, often with the hope that it will stay in the family and be appreciated by future generations, to delight or benefit others in the way it has the person who put it together. Wills I've encountered from the sixteenth and seventeenth centuries sometimes have a very particular legacy in mind, with books to stay exactly where they are on the shelves. Frances Wolfreston left hers to her son, but for the good of the family more generally; and Anne Clifford specified that her books 'may not bee removed or taken away out of my sayd Castles and houses, but may still remayne as heyr-loomes therein for the Good of my Posterity'. The collections of Clifford and Wolfreston were dispersed a long time ago, in spite of the intentions stated in their wills. Others have fared better. In the early seventeenth century Samuel Harsnett, Archbishop of York, left his collection of some 900 books to the town of Colchester for the benefit of the local clergy, and it remains there in the care of the University of Essex Library; others have become the founding collections of many institutional libraries.

What do you lose when a collection is broken up? Is it really more than the sum of its parts? Pulling apart a lifetime's work in building a collection risks losing the collector's knowledge, expertise and the connections she or he has made between books. For this reason I am glad to be a librarian, as we still occasionally see whole collections passing into institutional libraries where they remain intact. Of particular difficulty are modern academic collections, where the subject expertise is vast and highly specialized, but the books themselves are often neither rare nor valuable. Such collections are usually dispersed without a lasting record. Rarer and valuable collections (which sometimes lack a deep academic subject knowledge) fare better if they are sold at auction or through a single bookseller who will produce a catalogue and thus a record for posterity. If you find yourself getting rid of someone else's books, you might consider putting a label into some of them as a small memorial to the person who owned them.

Booksellers see the dispersal of a collection as an opportunity for new owners to acquire new things, and most collections are formed, of course, from the disassembled parts of other collections. Since few collections remain intact after an owner's death, this endless reforming of collections is fun for collectors, who have opportunities to buy new books, and for scholars, who have the histories of collections to write. If you become responsible for disposing of a collection, you might have a range of questions about it. Is there anything of value, and how can you tell? Would anyone want any of it? Can it go in a skip?

Sorting books

If you do have some time to sort through the books yourself, here's how you might start. It is good to make a quick list as you go, especially if you are thinking of offering them to booksellers or libraries: they will want to know what you have.

First, you might want to sort into hardback and paperback, and put aside anything signed as you go. Then look through the hardbacks, and see whether there are any obvious signs of a limited, first, early or special edition, especially of literature, poetry, children's books and academic books up to about 1970, and anything striking, such as unusual illustrations. The sorts of books that are most likely to have value are signed copies, first or early editions (in or near to an author's lifetime), limited editions, private press books, or books printed before about 1850. Pick out anything that looks unusual for whatever reason. Don't spend time on reference books from the second half of the twentieth century from big well-known publishers (for example, guides to things from birds to plants), or glossy coffee-table books, unless they happen to have an artist or photographer that seems particularly special or unusual. Bibles printed after 1850 are really not of interest to many people, so don't put these aside. On the other hand, don't discard tatty children's books, especially from the late nineteenth up to the mid-twentieth century, as there is a strong collectors' market for some of these.

Looking up value

Start by trying to ascertain whether the book is rare: look for it in a union catalogue of several libraries, such as JISC or WorldCat. When searching for a book in a library catalogue, use the Advanced Search function if there is one, select one or two key or unusual words from the start of the title (omitting articles) and combine this with a date or author surname in another search box.

You could also try a general search online, to see whether the book appears in an auction catalogue or sale. Beware of simply looking something up in AbeBooks or eBay, as, unless these are from reputable booksellers, the prices are often made up. An asking price is very different from value. Some auction houses have a sold lot archive, which can be useful, though even prices achieved at auction can be misleading if two bidders have gone all out over something they both wanted on the day. You might have to sign up for an account to access these. There are trends in book collecting, and prices do go down as well as up, so just use any price you find as a very rough guide, and have a bookseller give advice. It is probably quickest and easiest to have anything you suspect might be valuable appraised by an antiquarian or second-hand bookseller.

Selling

BOOKSELLERS

If you can't face sorting through the books yourself, some booksellers provide a house-clearing service. If you have substantial numbers and want it done quickly, for a minimum of fuss and without great financial reward, this might be a good option, and is a route commonly taken for specialist or academic collections. You should also consult a bookseller if the collection is mainly antiquarian (pre-1850). If you have just a handful of books that you suspect might be of value, you can also take these to a bookseller for appraisal and advice. Make sure, as before, that you consult a reputable one recommended by a body such as the PBFA or ABA. Some booksellers will offer a quick free appraisal, while others charge for this.

WEBSITES FOR QUICK SALES

If you are happy to sell your books yourself, there are a couple of options depending on the time you have. You could list them on an auction website such as eBay, if you are prepared to package and send each book away individually. If you want something a little quicker and less hassle, use a bookselling website or app. You simply enter the barcode into the website (or scan it if you download the relevant app), and are offered an instant price for it. I tried out a couple of these with Salman Rushdie's *The Enchantress of Florence*. webuybooks offered me 50p for it, and Ziffit offered 10p. In both cases, you need a minimum of £5 worth of books (or at least ten books for Ziffit) to go ahead. The websites are easy to use, but it's up to you whether you think it worthwhile to package and send off books in this way.

Giving away

CHARITY SHOPS

If money is not your main concern, charity shops take books and can often handle large donations. Some will even come and collect books from your home. Often, they are good at spotting valuable books: a Cancer Research shop in Dundee recently spotted a first edition of *The Hobbit* that had come in as a donation, and sold it for £10,000; a first French edition of *Alice's Adventures in Wonderland* was recognized at an Oxfam in Stirling and sold for £3,000; another Oxfam shop, twenty years ago, noticed a first edition of the first Sherlock Holmes story and sold it for £15,000.

Modern fiction in good condition seems to sell well, and a charity will get more for it than you would selling it on one of the bookselling websites or apps. While a National Trust bookshop might find it harder to sell academic or specialist reference books, Oxfam bookshops will be able to target these to suitable audiences; Oxfam also has a large online bookshop. It is worth contacting your local shops to see what will and will not be accepted.

PRISONS

The organization Borderline Books offers to take pretty much all books as long as they are clean, and redistributes its donations to prisons, schools, and to those fleeing war, persecution, domestic abuse, or without a permanent home. Books Beyond Bars has an LGBTQIA+ focus, and takes donations including English dictionaries and soft-cover activity books to offer to prisons. Give a Book also works with prisons, schools and other groups lacking books, and its website lists adult and children's books that it would like as donations in new or 'as new' condition.

SCHOOLS

Local schools might be grateful for some of your books, if you provide them with a list to choose from. The Children's Book Project serves over 300 schools and community groups; you can see all these on its website, and select one near to you. It welcomes children's books in good condition (no encyclopaedias, textbooks or religious texts). Otherwise, there are various charities that provide books to schools around the world, including: Book Aid for Africa; Book Aid International; Build on Books; The Book Bus; Books Abroad; Room to Read; Project Gambia; and Waterbridge Outreach. You will find websites for all of these. You could also try offering children's books to local parent-and-toddler groups, nurseries, or family or community centres, and other books to community groups and local care homes.

LIBRARIES

While you might like your books or your whole collection to go to a library, finding one to consider it will depend on the kind of material it contains. Academic, institutional or specialist libraries are best for rare or older books. If you have a connection with one – for example, if you went to university – that might determine where you start with this, though libraries will consider donations whether or not you have a connection. Francis Douce gave his enormous collection of antiquarian books to the Bodleian in 1834, but not because he'd studied in Oxford. In fact, he was Keeper of Manuscripts at the British Museum, but fell out with that institution and offered his books to Oxford, where it remains one of the most read and exhibited of the library's collections.

Sometimes it's simply a matter of working out where the book might be useful, and targeting your offer accordingly. If the book has a particular local interest, think about whether there is a local library that might like it. Specialist libraries such as the Brontë Parsonage Museum Library, Chawton Library (of women writers), and the Library of Mistakes (on financial history) are all examples of libraries that focus on particular types of material. There are things in favour of both small and large libraries when it comes to donations. A small library might lack the resources of a larger one, and donations could be especially welcome. On the other hand, if a book is of scholarly value a large academic institutional library will enable more researchers to use it.

When offering a small donation of a book or two to a library, do try to check their catalogue first, to see whether they already have a copy. Most do not accept additional copies of a book they already own unless there is something unusual about it, such as an inscription from someone of note. You will save yourself time and bother – and make your offer even more enticing – by checking first. If you are offering a whole collection, provide the library with a list of author, title, date, publisher, and any special features such as a limited edition number or inscription.

It is fairly unusual for a library to take on a whole collection unless there is something very special about it. If you are open to a library taking only those books that are of use to it, you will probably have more success in giving your books away.

EXCHANGES

Swap books you no longer need with your friends, or ask your local pub, village shop, hotel, community centre or place of work if you can set up a book exchange. Some people do these in old red telephone boxes, and I've even seen a tree stump in my local park set out with books. This could be as little as a single shelf or bookcase, or even a windowsill where people can help themselves and leave books they no longer need. If you are swapping, there is a cautionary tale regarding the Caxton advertisement I mentioned in Chapter 1. It belonged to Francis Douce, whom we met above. He had the only two known copies of it, and swapped one with Earl Spencer. He only discovered afterwards that the book Spencer gave him in exchange was lacking several of its leaves, and so of little use or value.

You could also leave a box of books outside your house with a note encouraging people to help themselves. This will depend on whether you are getting rid of your collection of Mills & Boon and want your neighbours to know about it.

FRIENDS

We don't make enough of used books as gifts. I went to a party once where the living room had piles of books stacked up for guests to browse and take home as desired. The 'buffet' mentality kicked in as I watched others browse, and I didn't want to miss out so took as many as I could carry while trying not to appear indecently competitive. Why not give presents of the books you don't need any more? Obviously this is not great if they are covered in jam or warped from falling in the bath. But, if not, how nice to know that a book was special to the person giving it, and that she enjoyed reading from the same copy.

I hope you will agree that there are alternatives to a skip when getting rid of books, even if it takes a little time and effort to find suitable new homes. By releasing books back into the world you are giving others a chance to find delight, solace or knowledge, and to create collections of their own.

End Word

It is easy to take books for granted. We've come a long way, from a time when they belonged only to a small elite such as Ashurbanipal, through the early ages of printing when books became more available to different levels of society, to a point where we can purchase from an enormous range of second-hand or even new books for less than the hourly minimum wage. We are lucky to have so many books available to us.

Of course, even now access to books is not universal. Books are unavailable to readers in many circumstances, whether the wonderful works of fantasy banned from some schools in the United States, the Ukrainian language books destroyed under Russian occupation, or the diminishing book ownership among children in the

UK (the National Literacy Trust reports 8.6 per cent of children have no book of their own in 2023).

The reason I love being a librarian, a custodian of books, is that I see how very long books last when well looked after. The paper on which the Bodleian's copy of the Gutenberg Bible was printed in 1455 is as fine and bright today as it was nearly 600 years ago, and turns with a beautiful crisp crackle. At the same time, I see how fragile books can be, and how easily whole editions, texts and authors disappear from our history. So, whether you turn off the water to your house lest it leak on your books, as one collector did in the twentieth century, or simply move them further away from the fire, I hope this guide helps you to delight in your books, look after them as best you can, and pass them on usefully.

Appendix

COLLECTING

John Carter, *ABC For Book Collectors* (Hart-Davis, London, 1952); now revised and on its 9th edition (Oak Knoll Press, New Castle DE, 2016).

Don Etherington and Matt T. Roberts, *Bookbinding and the Conservation of Books: A Dictionary of Descriptive Terminology* (Library of Congress, Washington DC, 1982); free online at https://cool.culturalheritage.org/don.

The Book Collector (London, 1952–). A journal with articles on collecting, and notifications of sale. www.thebookcollector.co.uk.

ONLINE CATALOGUES

JISC Library Hub Discover: https://discover.libraryhub.jisc.ac.uk.
Library of Congress Catalog: https://catalog.loc.gov.
English Short Title Catalogue: http://estc.bl.uk.
WorldCat: https://search.worldcat.org.

GUIDES TO FIRST EDITIONS

www.peterharrington.co.uk/blog/what-is-a-first-edition.
https://biblio.co.uk/book-collecting/basics/what-is-a-first-edition.
www.abaa.org/blog/post/identifying-first-editions.
https://blackwells.zendesk.com/hc/en-gb/

articles/4404788532498-How-do-I-know-if-my-book-is-a-first-edition.

BUYING

Antiquarian Booksellers' Association (ABA): https://aba.org.uk.
Provincial Book Fair Association (PBFA): www.pbfa.org.
International League of Antiquarian Booksellers (ILAB): https://ilab.org.

SELLING

Webuybooks: www.webuybooks.co.uk.
Ziffit: www.ziffit.com.

CONSERVATION

Harwell (largest facility in Europe, used by many institutional libraries including the Bodleian; can treat a single book or whole collection). Use for fire, severe water damage, mould. www.harwellrestoration.co.uk.
Institute of Conservation (Icon), list of professional conservators: www.icon.org.uk.
British Library guides: *The Conservation of Books*.

SUPPLIES

Shepherds, for archival polyester sleeves (brand name Melinex), rice paste, wheat starch powder, beeswax, decorated papers, bone folders, etc. https://store.bookbinding.co.uk/store.
Conservation Resources, for lead weights ('snakes'), foam book rests, etc. https://conservation-resources.co.uk.
Bodleian Packaging and Design Service (PADS), for custom-made boxes, envelopes, wrappers and book shoes. www.bodleian.ox.ac.uk/about/work-with-us/pads.
UV film for windows: many online retailers.

BINDINGS

Shepherds, Sangorski & Sutcliffe: www.bookbinding.co.uk/The%20Bindery.htm.
Temple Bookbinders of Oxford: www.templebookbinders.co.uk.
Designer Bookbinders: https://designerbookbinders.org.uk.
Fore-edge paintings: www.foredgefrost.co.uk.
London Centre for Book Arts, for bookbinding courses: https://londonbookarts.org.
Simon Goode, *Making Books: a Guide to Creating Hand-crafted Books* (London, 2016)

CHARITIES FOR BOOK DONATIONS

Give a Book: https://giveabook.org.uk
Books2Africa: https://books2africa.org
Oxfam, including its online bookshop of nearly 190,000 books: www.oxfam.org.uk
Amnesty International UK: www.amnesty.org.uk/amnesty-bookshops
National Trust bookshops: www.nationaltrust.org.uk/support-us/donate/national-trust-second-hand-bookshops

CALLIGRAPHY, ILLUMINATIONS, DESIGN

Calligraphy and Lettering Arts Society, with a list of its fellows: www.clas.co.uk
Society of Scribes & Illuminators: https://calligraphyonline.org
Society of Wood Engravers: https://societyofwoodengravers.co.uk/about

Index

association copies 18–19
auctions 42–5, 53, 172, 173
   catalogues 45–6
Austen, Jane 18, 28, 147

bindings
   decoration 26, 152–5, 156–7
   materials 26–7, 157–61
   rebinding 153–4
Bodleian Libraries 74, 126
   catalogues 47–8, 123, 127
   collections 15, 16, 17, 20, 22, 24, 25, 26, 29, 176
   conservation 80–81, 89, 93, 107, 109, 112, 113
   exhibitions 89, 91, 101
   librarians 23, 29, 45, 99, 103, 120
   shelfmarks 124
   storage 66–7, 81, 112, 113
   treasures 18–19, 28, 86, 95, 104
Bodley, Thomas 23, 29
bone folder 88, 114
book fairs 38–9, 40–41
bookmarks 97, 103–4
bookplates 141–3
booksellers 34–5, 39, 40–41, 172–3
   catalogues 46–7
   fictional 42
boxes 111–13

British Library 66, 93, 125
   collections 20, 22, 26
   treasures 56
Burton, Robert 17, 47
Bury, Richard de 74, 85, 93, 96, 98, 101, 143–4

Carroll, Lewis (Charles Lutwidge Dodgson) 10–11, 16, 136, 139
catalogues
   auction 45–6
   booksellers' 46–7
   history of 128–9, 131–2
   library 47–8
   personal 127, 129–31
censorship 48, 147–8
Christie, Agatha 8, 14, 15, 17, 19
cleaning
   books 92, 117
   shelves 70
Clifford, Anne 146, 168
collecting 6–8
   by artist 16
   by association 18–19
   by author 8, 15, 17
   by format 9, 14–15
   by subject 19–22
collectors 7, 20, 29, 30, 31, 40, 54–5

catalogues 131–2
condition 27, 38, 57, 59

damage to books
　foxing 106
　mould 80, 81, 82–4, 91, 117
　pests 93–5
　red rot 107–8
　water 85–6, 87–8

fakes and forgeries 20, 54–7
first editions 9, 36, 37, 174
　how to identify 10–14
Frankfurt Book Fair 39, 46–7

giving away books
　charity shops 36–7, 174
　libraries 176–7
　prisons 175
　schools 175
glues 109–10, 115, 116

handling books 101–3

illustrations 10, 16–17
inscriptions 18–19, 117, 135, 136–9, 170
　forged 54
International League of Antiquarian Booksellers (ILAB) 35, 42, 54

JISC Library Hub Discover 12, 21, 58, 171

Leonardo da Vinci 45, 52
libraries
　institutional 30–31
　personal 17–18, 29–30, 31
Libri, Guglielmo 52, 53

marginalia 27–9, 143–8
miniature books 24, 131

Naudé, Gabriel 79–80, 93, 100, 149–50

Oxfam 36–7, 174

prices 57–8, 171–2
prizes, book collecting 31–2
Provincial Book Fair Association (PBFA) 40, 42, 113, 173

Rackham, Arthur 16–17
repairing books
　drying 86–8
　paper tears 113–15
　spines 108–10
Rowling, J.K. 13–14, 15–16, 36

Shakespeare, William 24, 25, 29, 31, 146, 148
shelves 61, 63–6, 69
　arrangement on 71–2, 74–5, 119, 120, 121, 123–5
　rolling 66
storage conditions
　humidity 80–82
　light 89–90
　temperature 80–81

Tenniel, John 10, 16
thieves 51–3
Tolkien, J.R.R 36, 145, 158
treasures 155
　charity shop 36–7, 174

wheat starch paste *see* glues
Wolfreston, Frances 29, 149, 168
WorldCat 58, 171